Antique Furniture

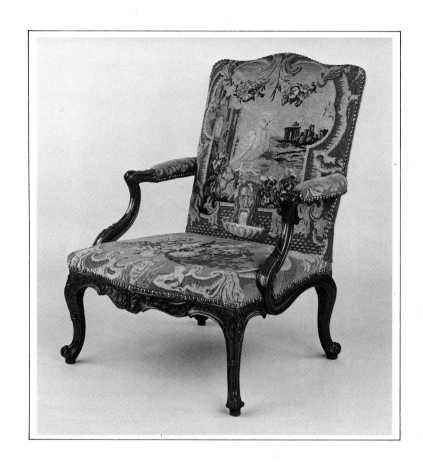

Antique Furniture

Baroque, Rococo, Neoclassical

Anne Stone

Foreword by Edward T. Joy

Exeter Books

NEW YORK

HALF TITLE PAGE Mid-eighteenth-century English mahogany library
armchair covered with *gros* and *petit point* needlework.

FRONTISPIECE Late eighteenth-century French lemonwood *secrétaire à
abattant* by Adam Weisweiler. The top is Carrara marble, the fall-front
decorated with a plaque of Sèvres porcelain.

BELOW A pair of *vernis Martin guéridons* of the mid-eighteenth century, the
circular *pietre dure* tops inlaid with butterflies and flowersprays.

© Orbis Publishing Limited 1982

First published in the USA 1982
by Exeter Books
Distributed by Bookthrift
Exeter is a trademark of Simon & Schuster
Bookthrift is a registered trademark of Simon & Schuster
New York, New York

ISBN 0–89673–140–5

Printed in Yugoslavia

Contents

Foreword

I N RECENT YEARS RESEARCH by historians both of architecture and of furniture has considerably widened our knowledge and understanding of the internal arrangement of the house in different historical periods. The ordering of rooms, the disposition of furniture, the part played by designers and craftsmen in these domestic arrangements and in the development of materials for furnishings have all been the subjects of major studies. It was in the seventeenth century, the period of the Baroque, that new standards of coherence and magnificence were first achieved in furnishings. The architects and craftsmen concerned have also been the subjects of careful scrutiny and their contributions to the changes in interior design can now be appreciated with far more understanding than was possible a few years ago.

State rooms were at first the creations of artists and architects such as Le Brun and Marot. Later, as materials became more varied and rooms other than state rooms came within the designer's scope, the upholsterer took over and his status improved immeasurably. In England after the Restoration, when upholsterers, under the direct impact of French and Dutch influence, began to play a leading part in connection with the luxurious furniture introduced in Charles II's reign, they changed radically from being dealers in second-hand goods and clothing to become advisers on house furnishings and thus, in effect, interior decorators.

It is the achievement of *Antique Furniture* that the author has provided a synthesis of recent research – for scholars, even when working on related themes, usually do so in isolation. The furniture masterpieces are displayed in a large number of colour illustrations which give the reader a general view of the best work of the period of the seventeenth to the early nineteenth centuries, covering three great eras: the Baroque, with its play on the majestic and the awe-inspiring derived from the classical legacy; the Rococo, with its light asymmetrical forms, when furniture reached a new standard of comfort related to the human figure; and the Neoclassical, the return to classical forms, first in the delicate, Rococo-

influenced touches of the Adam period, then in the more rigidly literal archaeological interpretation of the Empire style.

The countries selected for detailed analysis are Italy, France, the Low Countries, Germany and Austria, England and America. Each area has special factors, economic, social, political and religious, which have conditioned the making of its furniture, while all share in a common European inheritance.

Special attention is paid to the craftsmen who made the furniture or were responsible for the production of the pattern books which did so much to popularize styles. Text and illustrations both emphasize how important was the pervasive influence of cultured patronage allied to superb hand skill.

Edward T. Joy

The Settings

ETWEEN THE MIDDLE AGES and the seventeenth century, life in
Europe changed dramatically. The politically unstable and warlike
conditions of medieval society had been reflected in the battle-
mented castles and fortresses which were dotted all over Europe. In these
fortified dwellings, security was of greatest importance, and comfort was
minimal. By the sixteenth century, increased political stability led to a
corresponding increase in domestic comfort and luxury. But it was not
until the seventeenth century that interior decoration and concepts of
unified decorative schemes began to be considered.

In the second half of the seventeenth century, the centralizing policies
of monarchs like Louis XIV had successfully broken the power of the
nobles, and the courts of Europe had emerged as the centres of political,
social, and cultural life. The monarch was seen as the apex of an elaborate
court structure, and the brilliance of the king was reflected in and enhanced
by his surroundings. Once the monarch and his court had established
fashions and procedures, lesser nobles imitated them. By the last quarter of
the seventeenth century, the example of Louis XIV at his sumptuous
palace at Versailles set the pace for other European courts for the rest of
the century. The decline in the importance of the court in the early
eighteenth century in several countries in Europe, particularly France,
and the influence exerted by a rising aristocracy and *haute bourgeoisie*,
brought about a number of changes in both the arrangement and decoration of eighteenth-century interiors. But a few important features,
developed and established in the seventeenth century, continued to be
important throughout this period, the most significant of these being the
apartment.

Life in the seventeenth-century court was both formal and public. It
was rigidly controlled by an elaborate court etiquette designed to promote
and maintain the hierarchical structure of the court. Both the formality
and the hierarchical nature of the court were expressed in architecture
and in interior decoration. But there was also, although to a lesser extent,

RIGHT *A Baroque
staircase designed by the
court architect Filippo
Juvarra for the Palazzo
Madama. The palace was
originally medieval, but in
1718 Vittorio Amadeo II
of Savoy commissioned the
Messinese architect to
transform it. Only this
noble façade, which acts
as a screen in front of the
original building and
incorporates in its entirety
the grandiose staircase,
was completed. This has
led some critics to describe
it as a 'staircase without
a palace'.*

an informal, private side to court life and this too was reflected in the structure of the buildings.

The formal part of the house had a twofold function. It was designed to impress the public at large, and also to provide a suitable place for entertaining social equals. The very grand rooms were generally deployed in a series known as the 'grand apartments' in a private house, or the 'state apartments' in a royal palace, or in a house which anticipated royal visitors. The domestic side of the building was generally placed in a separate section or level of the house. The apartment was developed in France in the middle of the century, and was widely adopted throughout Europe during the Baroque period. The size and grandeur of an apartment was determined by the rank of the intended occupant, and it consisted of a number of rooms of widely varying size, linked together by interconnecting doors. There were usually at least four rooms, and in an important and large palace there were generally many more. These might include an antechamber for waiting in, a bedchamber, a closet and a wardrobe room. There was often more than one antechamber, and in a royal palace, the antechambers might also take the form of state reception rooms, such as throne rooms. Here, visiting dignitaries and foreign

ABOVE *Surrounded by her attendants, including a musician, and her pets, this noble lady, seated at her table, is depicted making her toilet. This picture clearly shows the deployment of furniture in a typical Baroque interior. The bed is placed centrally in an alcove and side chairs and accompanying stools are lined up formally against the walls.*

ambassadors would be received. In private houses, the number of ante-chambers tended to be less, though they were not necessarily any less opulent.

In this arrangement of rooms, the state bedchamber was the most important. It provided a central focus not only to the sequential order of the rooms in the apartment, but also, very often, to the house itself. It was generally the room through which all the main axes passed. The bedchamber in the Baroque household was the most important room of reception. Indeed, it was quite customary in the seventeenth century for the lady of the household to receive visitors while she was still in bed. The procession of rooms leading up to that most sumptuously decorated chamber provided a grand processional route which reinforced the hierarchical nature of Baroque courtly life. An elaborate structure of court ceremonial gradually evolved, which, by the reign of Louis XIV, had become entirely symbolic. The first public ceremony of the day was the *grande levée*, celebrating the fact that the Sun King was rising. The ceremony consisted of the gentleman of the wardrobe, who was always of royal blood, handing the king his shirt. As if to stress the importance of the bedchamber, Louis XIV's state bedchamber at Versailles was named after Apollo, the god upon whom Louis, as the Sun King, modelled himself. The bed was given ceremonial importance by being set apart, and placed behind a low balustrade in a specially designed alcove. This area was known as the *roualle*, and in a royal palace it had the effect of separating the king from the rest of the court. The importance of the bed was further emphasized by the introduction of a shallow daïs. In France, the bed was a most important symbol of kingship and authority. The canopy of estate which hung over the king's bed was a symbol equal to the canopy which was suspended above his throne, to which obeisance was required at all times, whether it was occupied or not.

From this most important reception room, a number of rooms led out, which were of a much more private nature. In France, these small rooms are called *cabinets*, while in England their equivalents are known as closets. They were designed for the personal and private use of the occupant of the apartment. They were invariably decorated in the most personal and luxurious manner of all the 'rooms of parade'. Gradually, however, these private rooms came to be used for receiving friends, and this re-inforced the increasing informality which was already becoming apparent by the end of the century. These small, secluded areas, in which the occupant could indulge his own whims and hobbies, and entertain his close friends, paved the way for the freedom and intimacy of the Rococo period.

While the state apartments provided appropriate settings for important visitors, the heads of families and their wives also enjoyed the comforts of their own separate apartments (marriages for love being rare, husbands and wives maintained separate but almost equal establishments under the same roof, each with his or her own set of servants and friends). Other members of the family were also accorded their own apartments, which differed in size according to the individual's status. The apartments were decorated according to the means of the owners, and though not every apartment showed the same degree of luxury as the state apartments, every modern convenience possible would be incorporated into the individual apartments. In Baroque houses, state apartments were placed on the first floor, while family and domestic rooms were placed either on the floor above or occasionally below them, or in some cases, in a separate wing of the house.

The dominant feature of the Baroque interior was its appearance of gorgeous luxury tinged with awesome severity. The formality of the seventeenth-century lifestyle was reflected in the strictly formal arrangement of the architecture, and in the deployment of the furniture. At the same time, the use of fabulous materials and exotic items enhanced the majesty and ostentation of the whole. But generally, this kind of luxury was found only in the houses of members of the nobility.

The arrangement of furniture during the seventeenth and throughout much of the eighteenth centuries was very different from furniture arrangement today. If we were to walk into a Baroque interior, we would first, most likely, be struck by the very lack of furniture, and then by the unfamiliar formality of its arrangement. From prints, engravings, paintings and literature, contemporary furniture historians have been able to reconstruct the interiors of long ago. The engravings of Abraham Bosse, depicting the interiors of the mid-seventeenth century Parisian *haut monde*, the designs of Jean Le Pautre and Daniel Marot portraying almost unbelievably elaborate bedchambers, and William Hogarth's English domestic scenes are of particular value for the impressions they give of the fashions of their times.

By the middle of the seventeenth century, furniture was no longer placed at random in a room. In France, and then elsewhere, harmonized settings were established, and furniture was recognized as playing an important part in the overall design. This signalled at last a recognition of the basic Renaissance architectural principle that an ordered and harmonious setting could be achieved through careful spatial arrangement. Although Italian Renaissance ideas had been familiar throughout Europe since the sixteenth century, they were never fully appreciated until well into the seventeenth, when people began to realize that this principle of harmony could be applied to the interior of a house as well as to its exterior.

Plans were drawn up for the arrangements of individual rooms.

RIGHT *Mirrors were a luxurious feature in Baroque interiors. They are used to great effect in the magnificent Galerie des Glaces at Versailles, which was designed by the two great protagonists of the early Louis XIV style, J. H. Mansart and Charles Le Brun. While Mansart was responsible for the architectural details, Le Brun carried out the decorated schemes for the gallery. The painted ceiling depicts events drawn from Louis XIV's reign. The use of marble and mirrors, and the elaborately inlaid floor are typical features of a luxurious Baroque interior.*

Emphasis was given to architectural features such as windows, doors, and fireplaces. In the *Mercure Gallant* of 1673, it was noted that curtains 'are now split down the middle, and instead of being drawn to one side, they are drawn apart to the two sides; this method has been introduced, both because it is more convenient and also because the windows look handsomer like this.' Doors were placed in corresponding positions in each room. This emphasized the processional aspect of the apartment, and allowed a distant glimpse of the wonderful rooms to come. Fireplaces were enormous, elaborately carved edifices, though they gradually became lighter with the introduction of Rococo designs.

Mirrors were important in both Baroque and Rococo plans. In the seventeenth century, they were often incorporated into grandiose mural schemes, the very grandest being the Hall of Mirrors at Versailles. By the second half of the century, mirrors were designed to match and complement pieces in suites of furniture. A suite would consist of a table, a pair of flanking candlestands, and a mirror. These were generally positioned against a pier wall (the wall section between two windows) and were known as pier glasses. Such suites became increasingly important, and appeared in grand rooms throughout the eighteenth century.

Sumptuous decoration was applied to ceilings and walls in the Baroque interiors. Ceilings, divided into compartments, were painted with grandiose allegorical schemes. Walls were hung with tapestries, brocades and silks, though in more modest rooms, wainscoting (wall panelling) still predominated. In bedchambers it was fashionable to line the walls with a textile which matched the bed hangings and seat upholstery. By the middle of the seventeenth century, chairs and sofas were not only covered in matching materials, but were made in suites. But despite this luxury and comfort, the formal character of the Baroque interior was maintained by the deployment of seat furniture in lines along the walls. Such formality was taken to an extreme in the French court, where a fine distinction was made between the *chaise meublante* and the *chaise courante*. The former was designed as part of the architectural scheme of the room, and was on no account to be moved. The *chaise courante* (literally, 'running chair', or one that could be moved), had to be created in order to solve the problem which this created, since people could not sit in lines along the walls and converse.

The widespread use of opulent and rare building materials also characterized Baroque interiors. Marble was used for floors, and for elaborately carved chimney pieces. In Holland, it was also used as skirting in the more important rooms. In countries where it was difficult and costly to acquire marble, such as England, scagliola was used instead, in many ways, such as for the decorative surrounds of fireplaces and even for window sills. 'Graining' was another popular decorative device. To make a local timber appear much more expensive than it really was, it was painted,

RIGHT *Mirrors played an important part in both Baroque and Rococo interiors. This octagonal room, the Spiegelkabinet (mirror room) at Schloss Pommersfelden was designed for the Prince Bishop Lothar Franz von Schonborn by Ferdinand Plitzner, and was finished in 1718. The carved and gilded walnut panelling provides a striking contrast to the inset mirrors, which reflect both the brilliant blue, white and gold stuccoed ceiling (decorated by Daniel Schenk), and the superbly worked marquetry floor.*

or 'grained' to look like another wood, such as walnut. Floors were also given special treatment, and inlaid parquetry decoration was seen on floors in Europe from the middle of the seventeenth century.

The introduction of Rococo styles throughout Europe by the middle of the eighteenth century led to a number of changes in the organization of rooms, and a corresponding change in their uses. Rooms continued to be decorated according to their different uses, the least important rooms being more simply decorated than the more important ones. Significant innovations were seen in the development of the salon and the drawing room. In the seventeenth century, the bedchamber had been the reception

ABOVE LEFT *An exquisite panel of carved and painted wood characteristic of the high quality of craftsmanship and artistic accomplishment evident throughout the eighteenth century.*

room, but over the course of time, the salon began to be used for large gatherings, and the smaller, more intimate drawing room (a development from the closet) was used for smaller groups. Another new feature which had only rarely been seen in the Baroque interior was the dining room. Formerly, state dining or banqueting chambers had been included only in the state apartments. The dining room became much more common in the Rococo interior, and two were sometimes to be found, one for informal, family use, the other for grander occasions. The arrangement of furniture in a formal dining room was again very different from the arrangement today. Chairs were placed, as in other rooms, in long lines against the walls, thus leaving the centre of the room free for ease of movement. In the event of a meal, such as a dinner party or banquet, small tables were brought in and set up. Occasionally, these were linked together to form one long table, but it was more common to seat small groups of people around the separate tables, particularly in France.

In the eighteenth century, ceilings and walls continued to be painted with scenes taken from well-known allegorical and historical tales, but these scenes became generally lighter than before. This is marvellously exemplified in the work of the great Italian painter, Giambattista Tiepolo, whose ceiling painting for the magnificent entrance-hall at the Würzburg Residenz did much to introduce lightness into this stately triumphal hall.

Lightly carved and moulded wall-panels, or *boiseries*, were introduced at the time. They were often painted white and picked out in gold, and gave a sense of great airiness and light to the rooms, which were generally stuccoed and painted in light colours. This type of decoration was particularly suitable for rooms used mainly at night, like bedchambers and salons. The light of the candles would then be caught and reflected on the light-coloured walls and *boiseries* by the numerous mirrors which were so often brilliantly deployed during the Rococo period.

Luxurious textiles continued to be used in Rococo interiors. But deep colours were abandoned in favour of lighter pastel shades, pink, yellow, lilac, and soft greys and blues and greens. Architectural features, even doors, were blended into the overall scheme of carved panelling, so that occasionally it was difficult to recognize where the panelling ended and the doorway began. And panelling itself no longer conformed to architectural conventions. The carved and moulded decoration sometimes interrupted corners, sometimes flowed in and out of the panel space, as though it had a life of its own.

Though the state apartment was still an essential part of the elegant interior in the eighteenth century, it was now generally on the ground floor instead of on the first floor, and was rarely used, except for ceremonies. The state bed was almost never slept in, even in royal palaces, where a less imposing bedchamber was generally concealed behind the state bed-

chamber. Even Louis XIV had been wont to leave his state bed after he was delivered into it, returning to it before the rising ceremony. His grandson, Louis XV, went much further, and had *petits appartements* constructed behind the *grands appartements* which he used instead of the formidable apartments built for the Sun King. The *petits appartements* were far from simple, but they were more comfortable by far than their Baroque forerunners.

Furniture, of course, continued to be of great importance in interior

ABOVE *In the seventeenth and eighteenth centuries dolls' houses were made as highly valued visual records of a property. In this model, one room has a panelled interior, and another has walls painted by the artist Nicolas Piemont.*

decoration. In the most formal reception room, the salon, gilded furniture lined the walls. Elaborately carved and gilded console tables were reflected in the magnificently carved mirrors which surmounted them. Superbly woven carpets from factories such as Aubusson were laid on floors which were otherwise left bare. The formal symmetry of the rooms was still maintained through the careful positioning of features like doors,

BELOW *A 'Design for the side of a room' by John Linnell showing a typical Rococo scheme for an interior.*

ABOVE *The Chateau de Champs was one of the many homes of Louis XV's cultured mistress, Madame de Pompadour. This, the Grand Salon, was decorated in the chinoiserie style by Christopher Huet in about 1758.*

RIGHT *This is the bedchamber used by the last queen of the ancien régime, Marie-Antoinette. The emblem of France, the fleur-de-lis, decorates the ceiling. The two chairs in the foreground are of Empire design.*

some of which were 'dummies' placed there merely to retain the suggestion of symmetry. Fireplaces had become much lighter in form, and they were generally surmounted by lightly framed mirrors, rather than by paintings, as before.

In bedchambers, both in private and state apartments, the taste for chinoiserie led to the introduction of hand-painted wall papers from China, which provided a colourful background to the furniture now designed in the 'Chinese' style.

Chinoiserie was not so fashionable in America, where the elegant houses of the mid-eighteenth century were modelled on the austere outlines of English Palladian architecture. Compared to European buildings, American houses were very modest, with smaller rooms and lower ceilings. Panelling was fashionable, and decorative devices, such as classical pilasters, alcoves and niches in which to display valued objects, were employed to great effect in eighteenth-century American drawing rooms.

During the early phase of the Neoclassical period in Europe, up to the end of the eighteenth century, Neoclassical ornament and an increasingly linear use of forms predominated. There was a return to the type of allegorical and historical painting favoured during the Baroque period on

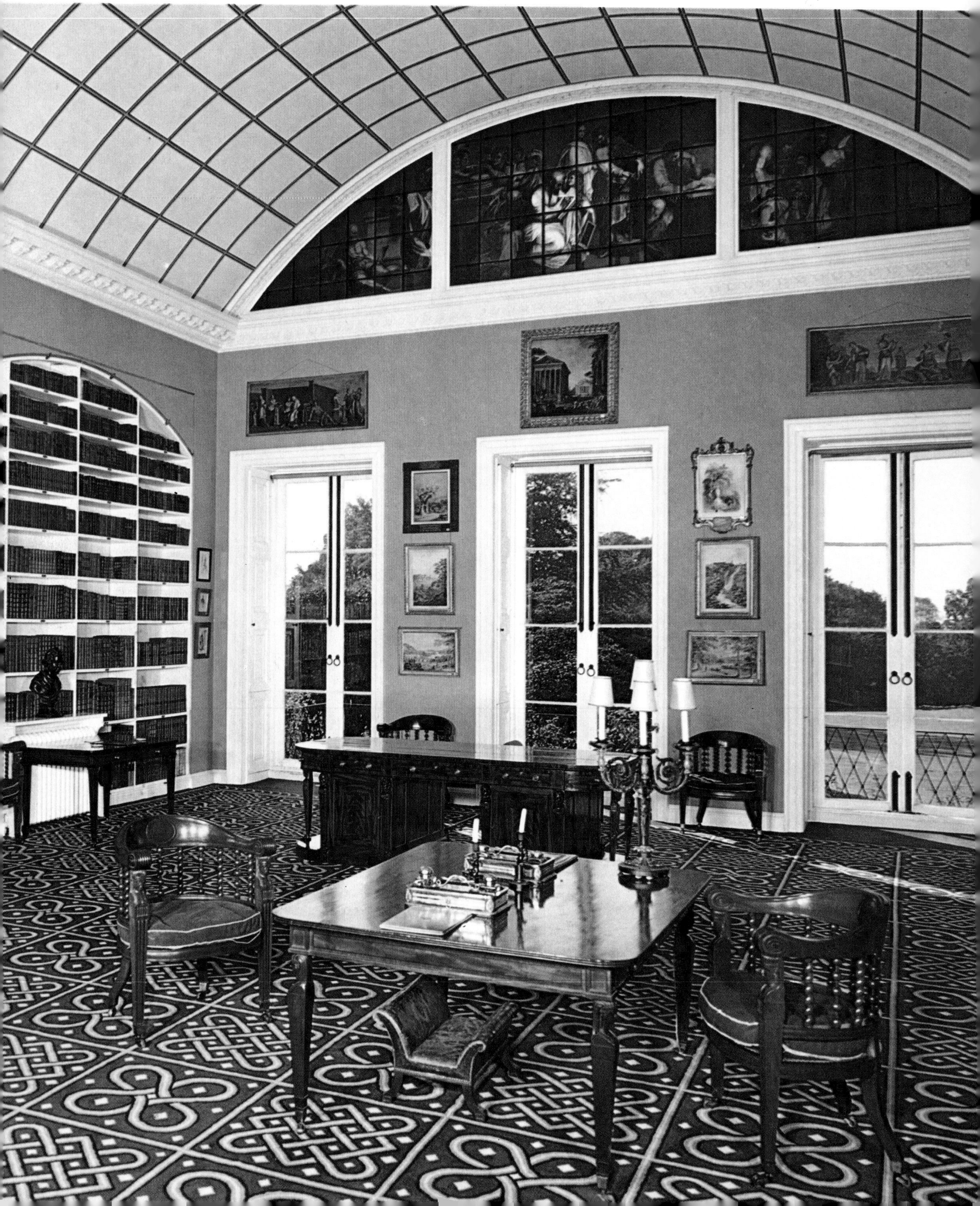

ABOVE   *This bedchamber, known as the Yellow Room, may have been used by the Emperor Napoleon when staying at Malmaison.*

LEFT   *The severe, masculine appearance of this room is typical of the style of decoration favoured for libraries by the beginning of the nineteenth century.*

walls and ceilings, and a new style of painting, imitating the designs on 'Etruscan' pottery, was also very popular, especially in England where architects like Robert Adam used Etruscan models to decorate entire rooms.

Superficially, there was little change in the arrangement of interiors with the introduction of the Neoclassical style in Europe. The importance of the apartment continued, although in some countries, like England, it tended to be on the decline. Horace Walpole remarked that apartments appeared to be old-fashioned, and another mid-eighteenth-century writer said that the rooms seemed to have 'little use but to be walked through'. There were more reception rooms designed for communal, rather than individual use in England (though not in Europe generally). Such rooms were libraries, dining rooms, salons, drawing rooms, and even music rooms, and by the beginning of the nineteenth century, these rooms had usurped the place of honour of the long established apartments. These rooms tended to have predominantly masculine or feminine qualities. In England, the dining room was seen as mainly being for men's use, and this was reflected in its decoration and furniture, while the drawing room and boudoir were intended mainly for women's use and were decorated accordingly.

In the eighteenth century, there was a greater degree of ceremony and formality in Europe generally than in England, but by the second half of the century, private life at least had come to be considerably more

LEFT *This picture, 'La Consolation de L'Absence', shows the cosy clutter which had become fashionable in France by the second quarter of the nineteenth century. The simple forms of the late eighteenth-century Neoclassical style can, however, be seen in the armchair (only part of which is visible), the enormous mirror hanging above the console table, and the table.*

The bedchamber designed for the Empress Joséphine in 1810 is decorated with the swan motif so dear to her, and which lends a feminine note to the Empire style. A boldly carved and gilded eagle proudly surmounts the bed.

relaxed, even in Europe. The reception of an important visitor was, however, still a matter of great ceremony, even in England. Mrs. Dalaney comments thus on her preparations for a royal visitor, one of George III's daughters:

> All the comfortable sophas and great chairs, all the pyramids of books (adorning almost every chair), all the tables and even the spinning wheel were banish'd for that day, and the blue damask chairs, set in prim form around the room, only one arm'd chair placed in the middle for Her Royal Highness.

The necessity to 'set the chairs in prim form around the room' was already regarded as an old-fashioned convention, but it was not until the nineteenth century that the relaxed deployment of furniture was actually considered acceptable. Smaller, more informal houses, such as villas, were also beginning to replace the formal 'houses of parade'.

But at the same time as a certain informality was beginning to be seen, there was also an opposite trend towards historical exactitude in interior decoration and furnishings in the Neoclassical style. In England, this was particularly apparent in the severely tectonic interiors designed by Thomas Hope, and imitated by many others. In France, the increasing stress on academically correct interpretation of Neoclassical forms was particularly evident in the Empire period. Recovering rapidly from the chaos created by the Revolution of 1789, France, under the strong guidance of Napoleon, developed an imperial style modelled on the classical splendours of ancient Rome. Under France's martial domination, the style spread rapidly throughout the occupied countries of Europe. Empire interiors showed studied simplicity in their severely classical decoration. Extreme attention to detail was one characteristic feature of the Empire style, one which had also characterized the work of Robert Adam in the earlier phase of Neoclassicism. Painted decoration in the form of murals, imitating antique mosaics or illustrating mythological scenes, was much in favour. Martial accoutrements were also introduced, and interiors were sometimes even lined with pleated silks, in imitation of campaign tents, as in Empress Joséphine's bedchamber at Malmaison.

The informality discreetly apparent in the late eighteenth century

BELOW *One of a series of rooms in Thomas Hope's house in Duchess Street, London, sketched by his friend, Flaxman. Each room in the house was decorated in accordance with a different archaeological theme, showing Greek, Roman or Egyptian motifs.*

LEFT *The severity of the Empire style was considerably softened by the use of fabrics and textiles, which were often hung on walls and furniture in softly flowing folds. This is a design for a bedchamber by Percier and Fontaine, and shows the style of decoration largely created and developed by them.*

emerged rapidly and openly in the early nineteenth century. The new informality was reflected in social mores, in literature, art, and architecture, as well as in interior decoration and in the arrangement of furniture. By the end of the second decade of the century, the careful disorder of interiors in both England and France (after the downfall of Napoleon in 1815), and the homely quaintness of the Biedermeier style in Germany, anticipated the cosy and more genuinely disordered clutter which would come to fill the rooms after 1830. Already, in the early years of the century, small tables were placed with studied casualness around a room, and people took to lounging on comfortable (though still elegant) sofas. Some pieces of furniture, like sofa-tables and certain writing-tables, were deliberately designed to be placed at random around a room. In her novel, *Persuasion*, written in 1815, Jane Austen describes the new fashion which was delighting the young and dismaying the old in England:

> The present daughters of the house were giving the proper air of confusion by a grand pianoforte, and a harp, flower stands, and little tables placed in every direction. Oh! Could the originals of the portraits against the wainscot, could the gentlemen in brown velvet and the ladies in blue satin have seen what was going on, have been conscious of such an overthrow of all order and neatness!

The Baroque Period

THE WORD 'BAROQUE' DERIVES from the Portuguese *barocco* meaning 'a rough, or imperfectly shaped pearl'. It was originally a derogatory term, coined in the early nineteenth century, and meant to indicate the innate superiority of traditional classicism. But by the middle of the nineteenth century, 'Baroque' was accepted as a legitimate artistic mode, and the word was also accepted as the appropriate term to describe the qualities, principles and forms of this dominant artistic style of seventeenth-century Europe.

Baroque began in Italy, which, up to the middle of the seventeenth century, was the cultural and artistic centre of Europe. The impetus for the new movement in art and architecture was closely linked with the counter-reformation. Baroque was the artistic expression of the Roman Catholic Church's new exuberance after the Council of Trent in 1563. At that convention, the Church had reaffirmed faith in itself and had called for new ways to promote and glorify Roman Catholicism. Sponsored mainly by the newly formed Jesuit order, Baroque was the art form which gave visual impact to the Church's new strength–for it was, above all, through the massively powerful and expressive medium of art and architecture that the Church spoke to the people. The Church's power was splendidly affirmed in buildings such as St Peter's Cathedral in Rome, completed under the guidance of the great sculptor and architect Bernini, in the powerful paintings of artists such as Pietro da Cortona, and even in the magnificent furniture of woodcarvers such as Brustolon.

Baroque art was essentially popular in its appeal. Its immediacy and inherent theatricality directed itself to the senses, and played on the emotions. Thus it differed fundamentally from classicism, which appealed to the mind, to the intellectual and rational. Baroque forms were designed to dazzle and overwhelm. Sculpture, architecture and painting were fused to create buildings, rooms, paintings and furniture which were sometimes almost dizzying in their magnificence. Chairs became thrones,

RIGHT *This early seventeenth-century monumental cabinet, designed in the form of a miniature palace, was made for Canon Passalacqua of Como, after whom it is named. It demonstrates the wide-ranging number of skills employed to embellish a single piece of furniture. The five ivory statuettes are the work of the sculptor Guglielmo Bertolotti; under each figure are painted copper panels by Morazzone, a leading Milanese painter who worked more in the tradition of grand decorative fresco painting than in these small miniatures.*

cabinets were miniature palaces. The grand illusion, of course, was meant to be shared by all, since the Baroque was, essentially, the Church's greatest tool of propaganda (as well as being the genuine dynamic expression of exuberant faith). But ironically, Baroque was a highly élitist movement, since only the very rich could afford it. It was an art which depended almost exclusively on court patronage of the most lavish and extravagant kind.

In an age when secular monarchs saw themselves as divinely appointed, the Baroque was soon put to the task of enhancing the power and the glory of the throne, as well as the Church. The splendour and power of Baroque forms seized the royal imaginations, first of Louis XIV of France, and then of his princely imitators in other European countries.

There were a few countries in Europe which were not ruled by absolute kings, such as the Low Countries, a few German states, and England, where Charles I had lost his head in the cause of absolutism. But even in these countries, the appeal of Baroque was irresistible, and they managed to adopt the decorative and artistic forms without the content. In the beginning, Baroque had been a visual affirmation of the power of the Church; then it affirmed the power of various kings, and finally, it affirmed only its own power as a form.

Italy

The Baroque was the last major stylistic development to emerge from Italy. Until the middle of the seventeenth century, Italy was looked to as the 'studio' of Europe. Rome was the centre from which artists and architects were drawn by all the leading kings and princes of Europe. Louis XIV of France looked first to Bernini to design his palace at Versailles. Bernini, the finest Baroque architect of the seventeenth century, 'was to Rome what Lebrun was to Paris', as Odom, a recent historian, said. Artists such as Tiepolo and Verrio roamed about the Hapsburg Empire, France and England, decorating the interiors of magnificent houses and palaces. But though Italy was the centre from which the Baroque spread, Italy herself was centreless, having been divided into innumerable secular and ecclesiastical principalities, dukedoms and city states. Italy therefore had no national Baroque style, like that which was developed in France under Louis XIV. But from the leading centres of artistic production in Italy, notably Venice and Rome, came a number of artists whose work was to have a profound influence on designs for furniture and for interiors throughout Europe during the first half of the seventeenth century.

Towards the end of the sixteenth century there emerged in Italy a number of powerful newly rich families to vie with the old orders of the established patriciate. The canals of Venice were suddenly lined with the palazzos of wealthy bankers and merchants. Genoa, which, through the success of her textile and banking industries, had risen to become one of the wealthiest cities of Europe, was filled with new palaces for the families of the ruling oligarchies. Florence, under the rule of the Medici family, revitalized the Pitti Palace and the Poggio Imperiale with furniture from the outstanding workshops of the Grand Ducal Palace. But it was Rome especially, having once more been restored to a new and powerful papal rule, which paved the way for a ferment of town planning, building, and decorating not seen since before the sack of the city by the French in 1520.

But as Lady Morgan was to point out in the nineteenth century, the palaces and villas of Italy's aristocracy were 'rich, stately, comfortless and showy, overloaded with ornament and deficient in accommodation'. The great audience chambers and the stately galleries of the princely palaces of families such as the Barberini, Ludovisi or Pamfili in Rome glittered with state furniture set amidst magnificently painted and stuccoed interiors. There were elaborate console tables with marble tops and huge mirrors, the size of which had never been seen before. There were superbly ornate chairs, which, if not as extreme in their decoration as Bernini's painted throne in St Peter's, were nevertheless undiminished and unabashed examples of the sculptor's art. Furniture of the period was most definitely designed to delight only the eye.

Italian furniture in the seventeenth century bore constant witness to the strength of Italy's sculptural tradition. The fact that much of the furniture was in fact made by sculptors rather than by furniture-makers is doubtless the reason for its poor constructional quality–it was created, rather than built. The furniture was heavy and static in quality, and overlaid with an exuberance of carving, of unrestful volutes, foliated scrolls, grotesques, and wriggling putti, interspersed with cartouches bearing armorial and heraldic devices.

Gilding of carved furniture was much practised, especially in Rome. Gilding was designed to set off the elaborate carving on such items as side tables, thrones, and beds. Carver and gilder often worked side by side in the same workshop. In Venice, there grew up a tradition of using, instead, natural coloured woods of contrasting colours and textures. The Venetian, Andrea Brustolon (1662–1732) was one of the finest furniture-makers of this tradition, though his elaborately naturalistic carved suite of furniture now on display at the Ca' Rezzonico in Venice is the only known extant example of his work. After Brustolon's death, the Venetian tradition was carried on by another sculptor-furniture-maker, Antonio Corradini, (1668–1752) whose somewhat lighter style anticipated the Rococo forms of the next century.

Architecture, too, influenced certain types of furniture, especially the

cabinet, which was invariably the most expensive and fashionable item to be found in a household. The twisted columns of Bernini's Baldacchino Monument in St Peter's Cathedral in Rome appeared everywhere– decorating table-legs and bed-posts, and flanking the doors of *armoires* and cabinets. The monumental pieces of Dominico Parodi (1668–1740), Brustolon's master and the best-known Genoese sculptor of the seventeenth century, are fine examples of architectural furniture. Parodi had been strongly influenced by Bernini, with whom he had served a six-year apprenticeship in Rome. Bernini's powerful theatrical style was reflected in Parodi's daring approach to furniture design, as, for instance in the outsize mirror and side-table which he constructed.

Mirrors were introduced in Italy around the turn of the century, and they became one of the most popular elements of Baroque furniture everywhere, since their frames were works of art in themselves, and the mirrors had the added glory of endlessly reflecting other masterpieces. Encased in carved and gilded surrounds of monumental proportions, they added grandeur and light to the salons of the Italian palazzos. John Evelyn, the English diarist, on a visit to the Villa Borghese in Rome, noted that a dramatic increase in the sense of perspective was created 'by the position of looking glasses, which render a strange multiplication of things

RIGHT *The Italians delighted in designing their cabinets in the form of sumptuously decorated miniature palaces. Cabinets were intended to stand against walls and so their frontal aspect was particularly well suited to this arrangement. Architectural motifs such as balustrades, pediments and columns taken from the classical repertoire were liberally used. Here the cabinet section employs costly and rare semi-precious stones, such as the lapis lazuli columns and exquisitely worked* pietre dure *panels, set within an ebony frame and supported on a carved and gilded stand.*

resembling divers most richly furnished rooms'. Techniques for perfecting the making of mirror plate were developed by Liberale Motta of Venice, and sheets of glass were made of a size never known before 1680. Crystal chandeliers and sconces were also introduced and popularized in Italy.

The grandeur of seat furniture was as much due to the rich fabrics used by the upholsterer, as to the massive scrolls carved upon it. Italy was well supplied with fine fabrics, as Genoa and Venice were the leading textile centres of Europe. The silks and brocades of Genoa and the richly cut velvets of Venice had been exported all over Europe since the time of the Renaissance. Beds, too, were upholstered with fine fabrics, particularly after 1650, when the gradual introduction of French fashions into Italy made popular the tester, or canopy. The more traditional Italian bed had four posts which often extended well above the bedstock, and did without the tester, which was widely used in more northerly countries. The posts, head and footboards were, of course, elaborately carved and often gilded, and some bedsteads were inlaid with semi-precious stones, in the fashion known as *commessa di pietre dure*.

Pietre dure was a type of mosaic inlay composed of semi-precious stones such as jasper, onyx, lapis lazuli, agate, porphyry and rare marbles inlaid in ebony or another stone. It was an art practised all over Italy, but by the seventeenth century, Florence was recognized as the leading centre for it. Small panels of *pietre dure* were generally made up of flat designs, portraying motifs such as small, chaffinch-like birds and delicate sprays of flowers and fruit, while larger panels were done in relief. These more sculptural pieces were particularly popular in France, which imported large numbers of panels during the second half of the century. Indeed by the beginning of the seventeenth century, there was not a princely house in Europe without an example of *pietre dure*. Very often, the panels were imported, and then made into furniture, as this was both more economical and safer (roads were bad, and highway robbers numerous).

The prohibitive cost of acquiring *pietre dure*, and the enormous popularity it enjoyed, soon led to the development of cheaper imitations. The most successful, called scagliola, was produced from a type of gesso made up of plaster of Paris, powdered selinite and glue. By the third quarter of the seventeenth century, this was widely used for table tops.

Colour played an important part in the decoration of Italian furniture, and in interior decoration generally. Lacquer, a form of decorative painting inspired by imports from the Orient, was much used in Italy from the end of the sixteenth century, particularly for decorating small items of furniture, such as tables and chairs. The chinoiserie designs done in Venice towards the end of the seventeenth century were of a higher quality than those produced anywhere else in Europe, and were sometimes done by leading Venetian artists of the day.

Italy was the unquestioned leader in developing and transmitting the Baroque style during the first half of the seventeenth century. In her abundance of rich and varied forms, she could not be equalled, and her very lack of cohesiveness was in part responsible for Italy's wealth of different art forms and crafts. The sculptural virtuosity of the Romans, the incredible skill of the Florentine *pietre dure* craftsmen, and the artistry of the Venetians were never to be excelled. But by the third quarter of the century, France, which had borrowed so heavily from Italy, superseded Italy as the leader of Baroque fashion, and began to pay Italy back in kind the great artistic debt she owed her. Italian craftsmen were enticed to France from the early seventeenth century. There, they picked up new

ideas from French geniuses like Le Brun, and took them home again. At first, French ideas only affected the northern states, since in the north many of the craftsmen were linked to French craftsmen through family ties. But gradually, French influence moved southwards in Italy, as it spread elsewhere in Europe. Despite the strong influence of France, however, many of the original ideas and forms of the Baroque lingered on in Italy until well into the eighteenth century.

France

The religious and political conflicts which tore apart the fabric of French life and culture during the latter part of the sixteenth century effectively inhibited artistic production from the end of that century until the middle of the next. The importation of luxuries from Italy, Spain and the Low Countries still provided the very rich with the finest fabrics and furnishings of the day, but proved to be a drain on the financial reserves of the country as a whole which it could ill afford. But thanks to the timely initiative taken by Henri IV, there was a gradual revival of the arts in France, which eventually stemmed this outflow from the national economy. Henri himself, however, was forced to look abroad for artists and craftsmen, with the consequence that during his reign France acquired a widely cosmopolitan culture.

After the death of Henri IV in 1610, his Queen Regent, Marie de' Medici, and the wife of Louis XIII, Anne of Austria, maintained the wide European links which Henri had established. Marie de' Medici, a Floren-

ABOVE LEFT *This prie-dieu in the form of a miniature altar is embellished with panels of* pietre dure, *a type of work done with particular success in Florence.*
ABOVE RIGHT *This type of small bureau takes its name from Cardinal Mazarin, who is said to have owned an early version. A simple provincial piece in walnut, it lacks the costly embellishments associated with court furniture.*
RIGHT *This cabinet, originally one of a pair, was made at the Gobelins in 1683. It is attributed to Domenico Cucci.*

tine by birth, but a devotee of Flemish art, imported a number of craftsmen from her own country and Flanders. Both Cardinal Richelieu, the power behind the throne of Louis XIII, and Cardinal de Mazarin, the most powerful minister during the long minority of Louis XIV, brought in cabinet-makers for their own purposes, including such outstanding craftsmen as Pierre Golle, Dominico Cucci and Philippe Caffieri. Cardinal de Mazarin was famous for the unprecedented luxury of his own household, but it was he, above all, who fostered the beginnings of a court art centred around the person of Louis XIV.

The most fashionable type of furniture in the seventeenth century was the cabinet, but it remained a rare luxury until the third quarter of the century, and was generally imported from abroad or made by immigrant craftsmen until about 1660.

The forms and decorations on cabinets (as well as on other case furniture) became perceptibly heavier and coarser towards the middle of the seventeenth century. Curves became more generous and more fluid. The work of the lathe turner dominated, with imaginatively rendered baluster, spiral, ring, bobbin and bead motifs. Moulding became thicker and more emphatic. Cabinets from Flanders, or made by Flemish workmen, were generally made of the newly fashionable ebony, carved in low relief. Typical are the two cabinets Pierre Golle made for Cardinal Mazarin. These large, ebony cabinets were inlaid with pewter, adorned with marble columns, and stood on carved and gilded wooden legs. Others, from Italy, were more architectural. Some took the fanciful forms of miniature palaces, enriched with inlay and marquetry of such exotic materials as mother-of-pearl, ivory, tortoiseshell, rare woods, and semi-precious stones and precious metals. More than any other single item of furniture, the cabinet symbolized the ostentation and extravagance of the period, which was so different from the marked austerity of the early part of the century.

The very high cost of ebony and its hard brittle quality were two factors which were to change the established concept of wood as a material. It was found that the only successful way to use ebony was to apply it as a veneer. This fact gave the impetus for a new category of cabinet-making in France, called *ébénisterie*, and the cabinet-maker, the *ébéniste*. *Ebénisterie* (or veneering) is the application of a thin sheet of wood on to a flat surface, with the use of glue and clamps. Generally speaking, the flat surface underneath, or carcass, consists of a cheaper wood, such as pine or beech. *Ebénistes* were responsible for making all pieces which were veneered, including cabinets, *armoires*, and bureaux. Other craftsmen, known as *menuisiers*, were responsible for making furniture carved from solid wood, such as seat furniture, beds, and screens. It was highly unusual for both crafts to be practised by the same person.

ABOVE *A detail from a tapestry celebrating the visit by Louis XIV to the Gobelins in 1667. In the left-hand section of the design, Louis is portrayed inspecting various items made at this royal manufactory, including samples of silver furniture and objets d'art, tapestries, sumptuous fabrics and several items of furniture.*

The death of Cardinal Mazarin in 1661 had far-reaching repercussions on the artistic scene in France, for it was at that time that Louis XIV began to exert his divine right, assuming control over every aspect of culture. For two centuries, France had drawn on foreign resources to replenish her stock of decorative motifs, and despite Henri IV's efforts to encourage the arts France had produced few native craftsmen whose skills matched those of foreign craftsmen. But Louis XIV had an overriding ambition to establish himself and his court in a setting of unprecedented luxury and grandeur. It was his aim to become a king among kings, and one of his methods of achieving this was to transform his surroundings into a kind of worldly paradise, which would be the envy of all Europe. In order to achieve this lofty aim, Louis XIV realized that a centralized system for the decorative arts, under direct control of the crown, was necessary.

RIGHT *This magnificent cabinet was made at the royal workshops of Louis XIV at the Gobelins and represents the highest quality of workmanship. Tradition has it that this piece was presented by Louis XIV to Charles II of England, who had spent a number of years in exile at the French court. The diversity of the design would have required a remarkable team of experts to work on the piece, involving* marqueteurs *and sculptors. Floral marquetry was a speciality of craftsmen from the Low Countries and wood sculpture was an Italian speciality.*

Ironically, it was Louis XIV's finance minister, Nicholas Fouquet, who, most inadvertently, paved the way for Louis' ambitious project to be realized. In 1657, Fouquet commissioned the architect, Louis le Vau, to plan for him an estate at Vaux le Vicomte. He established a complete system of workshops at Nancy, to supply his new chateau with all the necessary furnishings. It was to be the most sumptuous and brilliant building in France. The chief decorator was the hitherto undiscovered genius of French Baroque, Charles Le Brun. In 1661, when Vaux le Vicomte was almost completed, Fouquet gave a huge royal reception, so he could display his fabulous chateau to the young king. Louis and his court were honoured with a lavish series of entertainments, culminating in a brilliant display of fireworks. But Fouquet lived to regret flaunting his possessions before the king. Less than three weeks after the reception, Fouquet was arrested on charges of embezzlement. All his property was confiscated, and all his artists, craftsmen, architects, sculptors and composers were put under the direct patronage of the king. They were to work under the direction of Louis' new minister, Colbert, who had succeeded Cardinal Mazarin.

Then Colbert set about looking for a suitable place to house the workshops for all the king's newly acquired artists and craftsmen. He found a tapestry factory run by the Gobelin brothers, dyers in scarlet, on the outskirts of Paris, and acquired it on behalf of the crown. New buildings were erected and the old factory was converted to house the enormous number of different ateliers (workshops) necessary to furnish the needs of the court; these included ateliers for *ébénistes*, mosaicists, *ciseleurs* (bronze founders), painters, *marqueteurs*, and sculptors.

Colbert made Le Brun (1619–90) responsible for the administration and co-ordination of all the manufactories, which were combined and raised to the official status of *Manufacture Royale des Meubles de la Couronne* in 1667, with Le Brun as *Premier Directeur*. Le Brun's abilities were monumental. A great designer himself, he supplied all kinds of designs and models for the sculptors, engravers, goldsmiths, weavers and furniture-makers. He also co-ordinated the work of all the different ateliers. It was Le Brun's personal fondness for the restraining formality of classicism which was largely responsible for taming the flamboyant Italian Baroque style which had been so enthusiastically embraced in the first half of the century in France. Though nothing was made without the specific approval of Louis XIV, it was mainly through the tremendous energy, skill, and perseverance of Colbert and Le Brun that an official national policy for the arts was formalized which was to make France the leader of fashion in Europe, usurping the position which Italy had enjoyed since the Renaissance.

It was solely for the king and his court that the artists working at the Gobelins or the Louvre ateliers made furniture; for palaces such as Fontainebleau, Marly, the Louvre, the Trianon, the Tuileries, St Germain, and above all, for the new palace of Versailles. Output from the workshops was vast. Items included in the *Mercure Gallant*, which contained exhaustive lists of the new furniture at Versailles, were a silver throne, countless tables, *guéridons*, mirror frames and girandoles, and beautifully wrought tubs for orange trees to line the Grand Galérie (Hall of Mirrors) – all of silver. It was a degree of luxury never to be equalled in Europe. But the expensive wars undertaken by Louis XIV cost him all his silver furniture. He had to send it to the melting pot of the royal mint. Now, only a few silver pieces from England and Italy survive to hint at the grandeur of the age.

Many carved items of furniture were gilded or silvered, or decoratively painted. This was known as the 'Italian' style. This type of decoration was particularly applied to console tables, candlestands and chairs, which were often made *en suite*, as part of a matched interior scheme. Officially, gilding was discouraged, because its prohibitive costs caused a drain on the national resources, but the various sumptuary edicts which were passed to restrict the practice were notoriously disregarded, at least by the very fashionable.

Another brilliant artist and designer of the period was Jean Le Pautre (1618–82), the leading exponent of Le Brun. Le Pautre's naturalistic designs in high relief lent vitality to the type of classical ornament which had been popular ever since the Renaissance. His grotesques and beasts were imbued with life. Lively putti holding festoons, flowers, and swags were the order of the day, and the designs of Le Pautre, published as engravings, were much used by other furniture-makers as well. Other motifs introduced during the early Louis XIV period were the fleur-de-lis (still the national emblem), the sunburst motif symbolizing Louis' view of himself as *le roi soleil*, and Louis' personal cipher of two Ls intertwined. By the 1680s, however, the highly sculptural and naturalistic style of Le Pautre, Jean Marot and others had given way to a more delicate surface type of decoration, typified by artists such as Jean Bérain (1639–1711) and André-Charles Boulle (1642–1732).

Bérain's lighter style, which superseded the more sombre designs of Le Pautre, was the first tentative step towards Rococo in France. His preference for lighter, more delicate arabesque forms was shared by the *ébéniste*, André-Charles Boulle. Boulle's personal life was full of tragedy and disaster, yet his exquisite and delicate work displays anything but a morose quality. Boulle developed a style of furniture decoration which has since been given his name, Boulle work. Boulle work is a subtle combination of tortoiseshell and brass inlaid in ebony. Alternate layers of tortoiseshell and brass were clamped together, then cut out in a pattern and reassembled in complementary patterns. The first cutting, where brass was used as the background material, was called *première-partie*, while the reverse pattern was called *contre-partie*. Other materials were added to the brass and tortoiseshell: semi-precious metals, such as tin and pewter, mother-of-pearl (and sometimes real pearls), and horn. The tortoiseshell was frequently enlivened by backings of different-coloured foils. This type of work was much imitated by other craftsmen, and was applied to bookcases (which were just beginning to appear throughout Europe), tables, pedestals, mirror-frames, bureaux, cabinets, and clock cases.

Boulle and another *ébéniste*, Aubertin Gaudron, were responsible for much of the new furniture that began to appear during the latter part of the seventeenth century. One important item which first made its

appearance in France was the bureau, or table with drawers. Another was the commode, a type of chest of drawers which appeared at the end of the century. By the end of the century, the commode had replaced the cabinet as the most fashionable item of furniture in a household, and it was the commode which was to attract the greatest expenditure of talent, time and money in the eighteenth century. Other innovations, reflecting society's increasing inclination towards comfort and convenience, were small tables and *guéridons*. The *guéridon* was a candlestand, usually carved in the form of a Negro boy, and named after a Moorish slave of the time. It had the advantage of being easy to move. Other small tables were made with rectangular and oval or round tops. Games tables were also introduced at this time, many elaborately decorated in the manner of Boulle. And massive, elaborately carved and gilded tables supporting slabs of ornamental marble, reminiscent of the type of table favoured in sixteenth-century Italy, were supplied to the court by the *menuisiers*. Console

ABOVE *A stunning example of the artistry of André-Charles Boulle. Of brass and ebony marquetry work, supported by sphinxes, the commode is one of a pair originally executed in 1708–9 as part of Louis XIV's bedroom furniture at the Palais de Trianon. The form is derived from Roman sarcophagi, and is known as en tombeau.*

ABOVE LEFT *A detail of the Boulle commode illustrated on the preceding page, showing a graceful winged female figure in the form of a sphinx in cast and gilded bronze.*

ABOVE RIGHT *Guéridons, or candlestands, were among the lighter pieces of Baroque furniture. Generally designed as part of a suite also incorporating a table and mirror, these light pedestal tables were, in their most luxurious form, covered with beaten silver, but almost all have been melted down. This one is of wood, elaborately carved and gilded.*

tables with marble tops supported on pilaster-shaped legs, or legs of caryatid form linked by X stretchers, were carved with an astonishing degree of freedom and then painted or gilded. Their function, when placed in position against walls, was entirely decorative, and they were often designed as parts of elaborate and costly suites of furniture. The idea of a 'suite' of furniture, in which each item was intended to be part of a predetermined design, led to greater coherence in interior decoration generally. Other items in a suite of matching furniture would have been an elaborate mirror frame, and a pair of torchères, or pedestals for candelabra. Suites of this kind were often created after 1689 to replace the solid silver furniture which Louis XIV had been forced to melt down.

By the middle of the seventeenth century, seat furniture, also the domain of the *menuisiers*, was beginning to show the same curvilinear structure as tables, especially in the use of turned legs and stretchers. There was a general trend towards greater comfort in chair design. The winged armchair was introduced at the end of the century, and was an early prototype for the *bergère*, which was later to become so fashionable. Like tables, chairs were often elaborately carved, and important ones

were gilded. They were frequently designed for display in opulently splendid matching sets. Chair seats were lowered in height and made wider and deeper, though their exact proportions and uses were still governed by strict rules of etiquette. Towards the end of the century, chair backs became higher and more shapely. Arm supports were curved, and legs were carved in baluster or pilaster forms, or supported by caryatids and other mythological figures. Seats, backs and sometimes arms were padded, and upholstered in richly patterned silks and brocades, velvets and tapestries.

In the early eighteenth century, a series of designs for all types of furniture, many of which had appeared individually during the 1690's, was collected and published by Daniel Marot (1663–1752) under the title *Oeuvres du Sieur D. Marot*. Marot, working in the same tradition as his father, Jean Marot, Le Pautre and Bérain, was an architect-designer whose engraved designs were to have considerable influence on late Baroque styles in France, the Low Countries, and England. Among the designs he is especially noted for are his elaborate designs for beds. In these can be seen how much attention was given not only to the structural aspects, which were the province of the *menuisiers*, but also to the draperies, the valances and canopies, which were themselves almost sculptural in their highly dynamic arrangement. Marot's engravings generally illustrate the 'arrogantly ornamental' yet dignified character of Baroque furniture in the France of Louis XIV.

The reign of Louis XIV was the grandest realization of the Baroque ideal. But in a sense, he outlived his own absolute power. He lived to see his ideal of centralized magnificence succumb to the lighter, less ponderous style of Rococo. The rigid formality of court life at Versailles gradually gave way to a more carefree way of life. Even the old king, in the last decade of his reign, recognized that a change from the autocratic character of the *ancien régime* (which had become even more austere since his marriage to Madame de Maintenon) was, if not desirable, at any rate inevitable. Rococo decoration crept into the drawing rooms of France around the turn of the century, and had settled in by the time of the king's death in 1715. Although the basic structure of furniture was slower to change, the curvilinear forms characteristic of Rococo were already replacing the splendid symmetrical lines of Baroque furniture.

The Low Countries

Towards the end of the sixteenth century, the demarcation of the area known as the Low Countries took place, forming roughly what is now recognized as Belgium and Holland. The Southern Netherlands remained under Spanish domination, but, by the Union of Utrecht of 1579, the

ABOVE *A magnificent carved and gilded armchair, typical of the stately court furniture which might have been used at Versailles. The tall padded back and the seat are upholstered in costly brocade and the deep fringing, which has now faded from gold to a brownish yellow, would have provided a rich contrast. The severe outline of the carved, columnar legs is reminiscent of the classical architectural influence of Le Brun.*

RIGHT *A magnificently painted interior of a cabinet showing the high standard of Dutch workmanship in the seventeenth century. The subdued outlines of the stand are in elegant contrast with the brilliance of the interior.*

northern provinces of what was to become the Dutch Republic joined together in their fight to throw off the Spanish yoke. Under the brilliant leadership of William of Orange, the Republic of the United Netherlands (now Holland) emerged. During the seventeenth century, while much of Europe was torn by war and strife–England by the Civil War, France by the Huguenot conflict, and Germany by the Thirty Years War–the Low Countries entered a period of unparalleled peace and prosperity. The great trading ports, first of Antwerp and then of Amsterdam, became the banking and commercial centres of Europe, and constituted Europe's major links with the Far East. The artistic products of the Low Countries were the envy of Europe–especially paintings, silver objects, textiles and ebony cabinets.

At the beginning of the century, Antwerp, in the Southern Netherlands, was the most prosperous city in Europe. The traditional manufactories of the region flourished. The Flemish tapestry industry exported not only its products, but also the weavers who made them. By the middle of the century, many of these weavers had established manufactories in other countries, like Mortlake in England. Flemish leather goods, especially wall hangings, with their embossed, gilded and painted designs, decorated the walls of palaces and houses like Dyrham Park and Chatsworth in England, and Vaux le Vicomte in France. And while typically Flemish works of art (silver, gold and leatherwork) continued to be exported to England and the Continent, through trade with the Orient, Flemish cabinet-makers were stimulated to experiment with new materials and concepts in furniture design. For the first time, they had available working materials such as ebony, tortoiseshell, ivory, and semi-precious stones. As a result, Flemish cabinet-makers became famous for their veneering, which usually employed ebony, often carved in low relief, portraying (typically) Biblical scenes which were surrounded by elaborately carved, highly naturalistic fruits and flowers. Their products, during the first half of the century, were among the most highly prized items in Europe. The cabinet-makers of Antwerp were also the first Europeans to popular-ize a form of marquetry using brass and tortoiseshell. This type of marquetry was later adopted and further developed by the great French *ébéniste*, André-Charles Boulle, by whose name it is now known.

In the Low Countries, there was no monarch (though William of Orange almost propelled himself to that position), and it was the bour-geoisie, in both the north and the south, who dictated fashion. People were generally conservative in their tastes, demanding traditional forms of furniture which were designed for use as well as beauty. Much of the furniture made was of the type which had been used since the Middle Ages and through the Renaissance. The family cupboard, for instance, was the largest and most traditional item to be found in a Netherlandish

ABOVE *This cabinet-on-stand is veneered in tortoiseshell and its brilliant reddish colour is achieved with a backing of red foil placed behind the veneer.*

household. Throughout the seventeenth century it retained its monumental bulk of a cupboard above a cupboard, though by the end of the century, the lower stage was often replaced by three drawers. But basically, it was only the superficial decoration which was changed, as pattern books became popular, and their designs were found to be at least superficially pleasing. Panels, like cornices, became heavier than before, and were often arched; the columns which flanked the doors were

turned, or sometimes supported caryatid figures or heraldic beasts. Corners were interrupted, or 'canted'; raised mouldings on the panelling were shaped, sometimes following the outline of the external forms; and crestings were shaped and carved, though never to the same extent as they were later to be in Italy.

In 1649, Antwerp's key position as the trading centre of Europe was brought to an end when the Dutch succeeded in closing the mouth of the River Scheldt, on which the city was positioned, making sea access impossible. This abruptly opened the way for Amsterdam to enter into the period of her greatest prosperity. Due to the many links which existed between the north and the south, many of the crafts practised by the

ABOVE *Flower painting decorates this Dutch lacquered cabinet, which is supported on a very richly carved and pierced gilded stand.*

Flemish were also practised by the Dutch. But the Northern Netherlands were predominantly Protestant, while the Southern Netherlands were mainly Catholic, and the difference in religion expressed a temperamental difference which was in turn reflected in the furniture. Cabinets made in the northern provinces were less elaborately carved, more restrained and more symmetrical than those of the south. Dutch cabinet-makers were famous for their exquisite marquetry. The floral marquetry of such craftsmen as Jan van Mekeren and Philip van Santwijk is particularly remarkable in its delicacy and verisimilitude. The elaborate crests and bases favoured in the south were abandoned in favour of surface decoration.

Dutch silversmiths also enjoyed an international reputation. In contradiction to the general conservative trends in Dutch fashions generally, silversmith Paul van Vianen developed the 'auricular' style, a rather flabby type of ornamentation which suggested the formation of the human ear. (He had been inspired by the anatomy lectures of Johann van Jessen, when he had studied in Prague.) Auricular forms were used for table supports and cabinet stands, giving them a somewhat distorted appearance.

After the revocation of the Edict of Nantes in 1685, many Huguenot craftsmen from France descended upon the Netherlands, bringing their knowledge and skills. Most important among these was Daniel Marot, who became *chef du dessin* to William of Orange. Marot's collected engravings, when published in Holland, had a tremendous influence on taste in furniture there, as elsewhere. But it was not until William of Orange adopted French fashions that the conservative Dutch began to incorporate state apartments with state furniture into their houses. And shortly after this turn of events, in 1688, William left the Low Countries to become king of England. He took many of the best Huguenot craftsmen with him, and when he turned his attention to his new country, Holland's brief spell of brilliance on the stage of Europe was over.

While the aesthetic impulse for the Baroque came from Italy, to be consolidated in France, many of its techniques were developed in the Low Countries. During the earlier part of the seventeenth century, Antwerp and Amsterdam were like middlemen between East and West. More than that, the craftsmen of Holland and Flanders were the first to develop in Europe the skills of veneering, marquetry, and lacquering, which were to become essential ingredients of Baroque styles generally.

Germany and Austria

Between 1618 and 1648, much of what is now Germany and Austria was torn apart by the Thirty Years War, during the course of which countless buildings were demolished, and artifacts destroyed. In the second half of the century, the constant threat of a Turkish invasion from

BELOW *The influence of Italian late Baroque design was most evident in southern Germany and Austria, particularly during the early eighteenth century. This magnificent library at Vienna, designed by the Imperial court architect, Fischer von Erlach, is closely modelled on the Gallery of the Palazzo Colonna in Rome.*

the Ottoman Empire was a significant deterrent to the development of the arts, until Prince Eugene of Savoy and the king of Poland finally managed to defeat the Turks by lifting the siege of Vienna in 1683. Only after this could the war-wracked country begin to develop culturally and artistically. The Baroque in Germany and Austria therefore came to fruition later than elsewhere in Europe, and many of its great achievements came at a time when other countries had thrown off the formal splendours of the Baroque and become fully preoccupied with the intimate gaiety of the Rococo.

Germany was even more fragmented than Italy during this period. It consisted of literally hundreds of kingdoms and states, some secular and some ecclesiastical. Prince bishops, and to a lesser extent, prince abbots had as much influence on the arts as their secular counterparts, the main difference being that the ecclesiastical patrons looked to Rome for their inspiration, while the secular princes emulated the glittering splendours of Louis XIV's court at Versailles.

Austria was the seat of the waning power of the Holy Roman Empire, and Vienna, the imperial capital, became one of the most brilliant courts of Europe. The Schönbrunn Palace, designed by the Imperial architect, J. B. Fischer von Erlach (1656–1723), was built on the grandest scale. It replaced the palace destroyed during the siege by the Turks in 1683, and was in itself a jubilant monument to the triumph of Roman Catholicism. The great religious victory was further celebrated in a famous bed carved for the victor, Prince Eugene of Savoy, by Leonhard Sattler in the early eighteenth century. Now in the sumptuous State Bedroom of the Monastery of St Florian on the Danube, this bed is supported by carved figures of Turkish prisoners who, in their anguish, are reminiscent of the captives portrayed on the console tables of the Palazzo Colonna in Rome. The head and footboards of the bed are decorated with emblems of victory. The bed lacks a tester, which indicates further the Italian influence.

The principles of absolutism and the power of the Church were vigorously fostered by the great officers of the Holy Roman Empire–but the power of the Church was generally understood in a very secular way. 'Tis my opinion, things duly considered', wrote the prince bishop of Fulda in 1738, 'that there is no need of any extraordinary Vocation [for a man to be an officer of the Church]; for these Gentlemen enjoy everything that a man would wish for in a genteel Life. The House they dwell in is more like the Palace of a great King than a Convent.' The archbishop of Mainz, Lothar Franz von Schonborn, prince bishop of Bamberg and archchancellor of the Holy Roman Empire, was one of the most powerful figures in the imperial court. He had a passion for collecting. The identification of his ecclesiastical rule with an imperial lifestyle was mirrored in the gorgeous interiors of his palace at Pemmersfelden, built to his own designs. The interiors of some of the more striking rooms were done to the designs of Ferdinand Plitzner from Franconia, a leading cabinet-maker of the day who had previously worked in France. Plitzner introduced into the palace the concept of a harmonized interior. Thus in the famous Mirror Room, the furniture was made *en suite* to blend with the elaborately patterned and coloured parquet floor; the walnut-panelled walls were inset with hundreds of mirrors, and hundreds more mirrors sparkled in the blue stucco ceiling, unremittingly affording the archbishop visions of his own harmonious grandeur.

Augsburg was one of the great silver-smithing and cabinet-making centres of Europe during the sixteenth and seventeenth centuries, and indeed, the smiths and cabinet-makers there had been the first in Europe

BELOW   *A pier table and matching candlestands inlaid with silver and tortoiseshell with gilded details. The combination of metal with exotic materials such as tortoiseshell, but more often ebony, reflects the widespread influence that the style developed by André-Charles Boulle had outside France. This highly Baroque group of furniture was made by the silversmith Jeremias Jakob Aberell, probably aided by the cabinet-maker Heinrich Eichler, at Augsburg between 1714 and 1716.*

to use precious metals in furniture-making, and the first, as well, to work several at a time on one piece of furniture, uniting different talents. The ostentatious silver furniture produced in Augsburg was well suited to the German secular and ecclesiastical princes' tastes. But during the early decades of the eighteenth century, the popularity of the elaborately chased and embossed silver furniture declined, and hard-paste porcelain, developed by J. F. Bottger at Meissen, became increasingly fashionable.

That French influence was strong was particularly evinced in the popularity of 'Boulle work'. One brilliant craftsman who worked in the manner of Boulle was Johann Daniel Sommer, who had trained in Paris, and who executed a magnificent cabinet for Schloss Charlottenburg in 1684.

ABOVE *A lacquer cabinet-on-stand by the German furniture maker Gerhard Dagly. Dagly was one of the pioneer lacquer workers in Northern Europe and made a speciality of using a light, often white, ground.*

After about 1700, Dutch influence made itself felt, especially in floral marquetry and in lacquer work, which became as popular in Germany as it was in the rest of Europe. Late in the seventeenth century, the Elector of Brandenburg, Frederick William (1640–88), brought several Dutch artists and craftsmen to his court, among whom was Gerhard Dagly, one of Europe's most brilliant lacquer workers. In 1687 Dagly was appointed Director of Ornaments to the Elector, and his work was prolific. He made lacquer cabinets with matching stands, tables and candlestands. What was unusual about his work was the freedom of execution and great beauty of the chinoiserie scenes he applied, which were often done on white backgrounds. Frederick William's son, Frederick I of Prussia (he became king in 1700), had an entire room decorated with oriental porcelain and lacquer cabinets made by Dagly.

Frederick I was even more interested in the arts than his father, and in 1702, he appointed Andreas Schluter, a designer who was strongly influenced by the Roman Baroque, to design his palace at Charlottenburg. It is not known to what extent Schluter contributed to the designs of the furniture in the palace, but the furniture shows mainly French influence.

The influence of French furniture designers was widespread generally. Many French fashions were disseminated through publications such as Paul Decker's *Princely Architecture*, published in 1711. J. J. Schubler's designs for furniture, published in 1720, helped to further diffuse the influence of Boulle, and a workshop specializing in exaggerated forms of Boulle marquetry was attached to the court of the Bavarian elector.

The close family ties between several Italian and German families, as well as ecclesiastical ties, helped to introduce Italian fashions in Germany and Austria. *Pietre dure*, and especially its cheaper imitation, scagliola, were used to decorate the dining room at Schloss Favorite at Baden-Baden, and *pietre dure* craftsmen were employed in important centres such as Vienna and Salzburg from about the middle of the century.

Some of the German courts fell into bankruptcy as a result of the splendour of their palace schemes. But these palaces, whether of ecclesiastical or secular heads of state, were magnificent monuments demonstrating faith in the ideal of Baroque absolutism, in the divinity of secular rulers and in the secularity of the divine.

England

On 25 May, 1660, Charles II, accompanied by his brothers, the Dukes of York and Gloucester, landed at Dover, where he was greeted by General Monck and a huge crowd of his subjects. Amidst tremendous jubilation and ceremonial fanfare, he was escorted to London. 'All the world's

in a merry mood because of the King's coming,' wrote Samuel Pepys in his diary a few days later.

The grey, austere days of Cromwell's Interregnum were gone forever, and as John Evelyn noted in his diary, the Restoration of the King 'brought in a politer way of living'. The period of Cromwellian rule in England had effectively arrested artistic production, as it had been official policy to discourage art and patronage. Cromwell's austerity had been reflected everywhere in everything. Furniture had become plainer, sumptuous brocades and velvets had been abandoned in favour of more utilitarian fabrics like leather, and bright colours and complicated patterns had been replaced by more sombre decoration, in keeping with the puritanical mood of the time.

The return of Charles II signalled a tremendous revival of art and patronage. There was a strong sense of renewed confidence and optimism, which was reflected as much in furniture and architecture as in other aspects of court and social life. The king's and his supporters' years of exile at the French and the Dutch courts and in Italy had given them a chance to assimilate the fashions and tastes of the day. When they returned to England, they brought with them a vision of the exuberant sculptural forms characteristic of Italian Baroque which were quickly adapted to the more insular tastes of the English. Carving techniques were imported from Holland, and chairs were newly decorated with gaily carved and

RIGHT *A headboard of crimson damask which was once part of the furniture for the state bedroom at Chatsworth. The work of Francis Lapierre, an upholsterer of French origin, it is one of the finest examples of English late seventeenth-century upholstery. The elaborate design shows the influence of Daniel Marot, a Huguenot employed as court architect to William III.*

pierced crests and stretchers; foliage and flowers naturalistically carved in the manner of craftsmen like Grinling Gibbons embellished stands, and scrolls enlivened small tables (candlestands) and chairs. The 'politer way of living' which Evelyn had marked upon at the start of the reign soon gave way to what he called 'luxury and intolerable expense' as King Charles inexorably gathered to himself the appurtenances of royalty. Courtiers and aristocrats soon followed suit. Charles' mistress, the Duchess of Portland, was particularly noted for the luxury of her apartments at Whitehall Palace, which surpassed in splendour even those of the queen. Interiors glittered with silver and gold mirrors, made *en suite* with tables and candlestands. Walls and ceilings displayed the works of the most brilliant painters and stuccoists of the day, and fabrics and textiles were elaborately fashioned.

At the same time that England was establishing a constitutional monarchy, a number of rich private citizens began to build their houses on a palatial scale. Petworth, Knole, Ham House and Chatsworth were among the finest of these. Though immensely luxurious by English standards, they lacked the extravagant excesses and verve of the Italian palazzi or of the glittering interiors of Louis XIV's palace at Versailles.

From the time of the Restoration, trade with the Far East was to have a tremendous impact on the tastes and fashions of seventeenth and eighteenth century England. This was largely the result of Charles' marriage, in 1661, to a princess of the Royal Portuguese household, Catherine of Braganza. In her marriage dowry were the promise of half a million pounds' worth of gold, the ports of Tangiers and Bombay, and permission for the English to share the Portuguese trade with Brazil and the East Indies. This last was a glitteringly valuable concession. The gold never materialized, but the trading rights in the East brought untold riches to England.

Caning, especially as used on chair backs and seats, was one of the innovations brought about by trade with the Far East. Caning was a highly specialized craft, and cane-chair-makers were entitled to set up their own shops to meet the increasing demand for high-backed chairs. Caning was popular particularly in court circles. The Countess of Dysart had several sets of caned furniture made for her magnificent house at Ham in Surrey, but only a few remnants survive, for caning is fragile.

Another type of 'India ware' to become widely popular after Charles' return was lacquer work. 'India ware' was a misnomer carried over from the early sixteenth century, when people believed that all things oriental came from India. Although there is some evidence that lacquer work had been known in England since the previous century, it was not until the Restoration that it enjoyed popularity. Like caning, lacquer work represented the exoticism of the East which fascinated Europe at the time.

ABOVE *This visual feast typifies the* trompe l'oeil *illusionism fashionable in late seventeenth- and early eighteenth-century Baroque interiors throughout Europe. Known as the Heaven Room, this is the climax of a suite of rooms in the great Elizabethan mansion, Burghley House. It was redecorated in the late seventeenth century by the fifth Earl of Exeter and much of the painting was executed by the famous Italian painter Antonio Verrio, who specialized in this kind of scheme.*

Some fine original examples of lacquerware were the magnificently lacquered cabinets brought to England by Catherine of Braganza in her dowry. Mounted on superbly carved and silvered or gilded stands, these pieces were intended for display in the finest rooms of the house. But oriental lacquerwork was expensive, so there were many attempts to imitate it locally. In 1688, the best exposition on how to imitate lacquer was published in the short *Treatise on Japanning and Varnishing*, by John Stalker and George Parker. The book was an immediate success. One respect in which imitation lacquer differed from the original was in its material makeup. True oriental lacquer could only be made in those countries (China, Japan, Malaysia) where the 'lac' tree, or *Rhus verni-cifera* was grown. Generally speaking, imitation lacquer was also easy to distinguish from the real thing by the comparative crudeness of its execution. But by the end of the century, this had changed, and many fine examples of indigenous japanning had been turned out by craftsmen such as Gerrit Jensen, a superb cabinet-maker who had immigrated to England from Flanders. At the height of its popularity, japanning was used to

decorate every kind of furniture–daybeds, tables, mirror-frames, and clock-cases. In a few houses, such as Hampton Court and Chatsworth, whole rooms were panelled in it. Lacquered and japanned furniture remained fashionable until the early eighteenth century, when its popularity began to wane.

King Charles died in 1685, and was succeeded by his younger brother, James II. James wanted a return to an absolutist type of monarchy, and this fact, his papist tendencies and various other factors led to his rapid downfall.

No dramatic change in English taste took place upon the accession of William of Orange and Mary (daughter of James II) to the throne, following the hurried flight of James II and Queen Mary of Modena in 1688. William was a paradoxical figure. A brilliant general, he was also a hunchback; a king who revelled in the glorious appurtenances of kingship, he was also a social recluse. He moved his court out of London to Hampton Court to get away from the social scene, yet he and Mary endeavoured to establish at Hampton Court a court as lavishly splendid as that of Louis XIV at Versailles. Unlike Louis XIV, William and Mary were dependent on parliamentary grants, and their projects had necessarily to be on a more modest scale. But if their hands were tied by parliamentary purse strings, a number of developments nevertheless took place during their reign which were to influence general trends in furniture design.

Mary was famous in her own day for her interest in (and collection of) Chinese porcelain, and oriental cabinets, many of which she had acquired from the East India Company. But Mary died of smallpox when she was only thirty-two, and William continued to reign alone until his death in 1701.

The most important single event affecting the development of furniture during William and Mary's reign actually took place before their accession to the throne. It was the revocation of the Edict of Nantes in 1685 – an act which was to have an instant effect on the culture of much of Europe. The Edict of Nantes had afforded the Huguenot (Protestant) population of France some degree of protection from the missionary zeal of the Jesuit Inquisition. After Louis XIV revoked it, many Huguenots fled to Protestant centres, such as Holland, and some went to England. Many more flocked to England from Holland with the Prince of Orange, when he agreed to become the king of England.

In his entourage was the Huguenot Daniel Marot. Marot had been a highly successful designer and engraver for Louis XIV, and then had made his mark in Holland after the revocation. As principal designer and architect to William III, he made several trips to England, principally to work on royal projects, such as the gardens and some of the interiors of Hampton

ABOVE *This japanned cabinet-on-stand is typical of the florid Baroque style fashionable in England in the 1670s. Not long after the introduction of lacquered furniture from the East, cheaper imitations were being made in England.*

Court. His flamboyant style had immense influence on English decorative styles at the turn of the century, on designs for beds, chairs, stools, and tables. His influence was especially marked on upholstered pieces, for his flamboyant use of rich materials in furniture design was strikingly attractive, and readily imitable.

During the last quarter of the century, the introduction of veneering from the continent affected furniture-making in England in several ways. A technique developed first in Italy, and taken up in both France and the Low Countries, veneering became really popular in England only after the accession of William and Mary. There had been cabinet-makers (the English equivalents of *ébénistes* in France, the term 'cabinet-maker' refers specifically to a furniture-maker who specializes in veneering) in England since the Restoration of Charles II, but they had been few, and had worked primarily for the court. The great increase in the number of craftsmen generally in England after 1685 meant a commensurate increase in the number of cabinet-makers, and European styles and techniques of veneering quickly spread throughout the country.

Veneering (the application with glue of a thin sheet of wood on to a flat surface of cheaper wood) led, quite naturally, to marquetry (the placing together of veneered pieces in various patterns). With the influx of so many skilled artists and craftsmen, several kinds of marquetry were developed in England. There was floral marquetry, reminiscent of Dutch still-life and flower paintings (and of course of Dutch floral marquetry!) There was oysterwork, the placing together of crosscuts from small branches in fanlike patterns. There was parquetry, in which pieces of wood were cut into cubes and geometric shapes. And there was, towards the end of the century, seaweed marquetry, the most strikingly delicate of them all. Seaweed marquetry was the development of the brilliant Flemish immigrant cabinet-maker, Gerrit Jensen. His technique derived from Boulle's, in France. But Jensen replaced the brass and tortoiseshell used by Boulle with different materials – usually different types of wood, both imported and indigenous, to give a seaweed-like effect.

In general, during the reign of William and Mary, a strong French influence predominated, after the more ebullient Italianate extravagances of Charles II's reign. There was, during the time of William, a discernible reversion to classical influences and to more defined architectural forms generally.

This trend towards greater formality was even more apparent during Queen Anne's reign. Queen Anne was crowned in 1702, and her reign marked a transition between the florid forms of early English Baroque and the formalism of the classical, highly architectural style of the Palladians. Furniture forms gradually became simpler, with more emphasis on graceful and harmonious outlines. Plain veneering was used for

RIGHT *A magnificent walnut cabinet decorated with floral marquetry made to commemorate the marriage of a Yorkshire couple, George Lawson and Margaret Trotter, whose entwined monograms may be seen on the doors. Although the type of arabesque marquetry associated with leading craftsmen such as Jensen was more fashionable at the turn of the eighteenth century, this type of delicate floral marquetry may be the work of a provincial cabinet-maker following the London style of a few years before.*

LEFT *Writing tables of this type were not introduced into England until the end of the seventeenth century. They incorporated sloping tops supported on legs which would swing forward, and which were generally made of walnut. Occasionally such desks were decorated with the elaborate and very expensive seaweed or arabesque pattern of marquetry. This piece is probably by Gerrit Jensen, a cabinet-maker specializing in marquetry who was patronised by King William III.*

surface decoration, replacing the more elaborate forms of veneering such as marquetry, and heavy carving was out of fashion.

One innovation was the cabriole leg, which made it possible to do away with stretchers on legged furniture. The word 'cabriole' comes from the Italian *capriole*, the hind leg of a goat. Sometimes these legs mysteriously ended in claws and balls, sometimes they were more appropriately finished off with hooves, or again they sometimes had scroll or paw feet. After 1710, the claw and ball foot became popular in England. It is meant to represent the claw of the Imperial Chinese Dragon clutching a pearl.

Another form which typified the Queen Anne period was the splat back or central panel on chairs. Early examples of the panel were in the shapes of slightly curved vases, while later examples were more ornately curved.

Lacquer work was still popular on case furniture. But there was a new type of gilt furniture, which became even more popular with the very rich: the gilding was applied on a gesso (a type of plaster of Paris) ground. Unlike wood, gesso was very easy to carve, and highly decorative patterns were easy to achieve, most popular of which were elaborate patterns of arabesque (flat lines of decoration). Firms like Gumley and Moore specialized in making most sumptuous furniture with gessoed carving.

Prosperity marked Queen Anne's reign, and with prosperity came the greater mobility of the wealthy. The gentry had country houses, and ideas were readily disseminated as people visited one another's grand houses. It was the era of the coffee house, of the gaming table, of increasing leisure, pleasure, and freedom. When Queen Anne died in 1714, she was followed by a prince of the German House of Hanover, George I. His court was German, he spoke no English, and he and his courtiers kept to themselves, and exerted little influence on English culture. Leadership in the arts was taken over completely by the aristocracy, as had anyway been the tendency in England.

During the eighteenth century, the prosperity which had characterized the reign of Queen Anne continued, and a new pursuit of education and culture flourished. It became the fashion for young aristocrats to round off their educations with grand tours of Europe. Among those who did the grand tour were the future earls of Burlington and Leicester. On their separate travels to Italy (which was considered the most important country to visit) they each met the designer-craftsman, William Kent, who had made his way to Italy from England some twelve years earlier. Kent returned to England with Burlington in 1719, having become his fast friend. Under the patronage of Burlington and Leicester, Kent was to

LEFT *The green velvet bed at Houghton Hall was made to the designs of William Kent for the Prime Minister, Sir Robert Walpole, one of the most important English patrons in the early eighteenth century. Bills extant show that the upholstery alone, which was provided in 1732 by the London firm of Turner Hill, and Pitter in the Strand, amounted to £1,219 3s 11d.*

BELOW *A settee probably made to a design by the Palladian architect William Kent. The ponderous form and the elaborate carving and gilding show the influence of seventeenth-century Italian Baroque style on Kent, who from 1710 to 1719 worked in Italy.*

become the leading designer of the Palladian movement in England. The Palladian movement was an artistic reaction against the extravagances of the Baroque, favouring a return to the formal, classic lines of Roman architecture. It had its roots in the published architectural drawings and writings of the sixteenth-century Renaissance architect, Andrea Palladio, and ultimately in the works of the ancient Roman architect Vitruvius. Generally speaking, it was the Whigs who embraced the Palladian ideal, whereas the Tories preferred the Baroque forms which by that time were seen as 'traditional'. Buildings such as Houghton and Holkham Hall in Norfolk exemplified the Palladian ideal, and Kent was responsible for much of the work on both of them. But Kent, like the other Palladians, though he knew a great deal about Roman architecture, had little knowledge of the sort of furniture which the ancient Romans had used. And having spent nearly ten years in Venice, Kent was heavily influenced by the work of sculptor–furniture-makers like Corradini and Brustolon. Their heavy, sculptural forms suited the Palladian love of grandeur, if not of simplicity. Thus, inside their severely classical buildings, the Palladians placed great side and console tables, heavily carved and gilded in a manner reminiscent of the massive tables which had decorated the galleries of seventeenth-century Italian palaces, newly made to Kent's ebullient designs. The furniture of this period, approximately 1715–40, was, oddly enough, some of the grandest furniture of

the Baroque style produced in England at any time, in its monumentality of conception and execution, its richness of carving and gilding, and its flamboyant ostentation.

North America

The opening decades of the seventeenth century saw the beginnings of the colonization of the New World. Life for the early settlers was full of hardship and fraught with danger. They had to cope with the problems of survival in an uncharted, often hostile environment, and had little time to spare for making any but the barest necessities. They had been able to carry with them on their voyages only the simplest tools, and essentials such as seed for planting in the spring. The wood-and-sod huts the settlers had to construct and live in must have seemed bleak indeed compared to the solid, if modest, houses they had left behind. Even more marked was the contrast between their new dwellings and the opulently luxurious and lavishly furnished palaces and country houses of Europe.

Few of the belongings of these early settlers now survive, but without any doubt their furniture was of the most basic nature. It was not until the second half of the century, when increasingly stable communities were springing up all along the eastern seaboard, that furniture-makers, local carpenters really, started to make furniture which, though primarily

ABOVE *A monumental carved and gilded centre table, designed by William Kent for Wanstead House, Essex and now in the state dining room at Chatsworth, Derbyshire.*

ABOVE RIGHT *Side tables were important pieces of furniture intended for display and generally used in state rooms, as this monumental piece, designed by Mathias Lock in about 1740, suggests.*

BELOW RIGHT *Card tables were fashionable items of furniture in the eighteenth century, and were often enlivened by elaborate carving, as seen in this mahogany example of about 1740.*

functional, was less crude and more decorative. By the end of the century, it is probable that every community of any size had a resident joiner, or at least a carpenter. The earliest piece of furniture that can be assigned to a maker probably dates from around 1680. It is a simple oak chest of drawers made by one Nicholas Disbrowe, who carved into the lower drawer, 'Mary Allyns Chistt Cutte and Joyned by Nick: Disbrowe'.

Much of the furniture made at this time recalled the predominantly English and Dutch origins of the settlers, being modelled on earlier Jacobean middle-class styles, a few relics of which had made the journey to America. Such pieces tended to be heavy in appearance, and were decorated, when at all, with motifs such as arcaded and moulded panelling, enclosing strapwork designs and lozenge shapes. The leaders of the various New England communities, who often came from relatively well-to-do backgrounds, were likely to acquire the more elaborate pieces, like the Staniford family chest, probably made in Ipswich, Massachusetts, which is dated 1678. This is a typical example of chests of drawers from that region, on which rich, contrasting effects were achieved through the use of different-coloured woods, and split baluster ornaments were ebonized in the style of early Flemish decoration. Geometric patterns were combined with painted and shallowly carved floral decorations (themselves extremely geometric in their precise forms), and on several chests and chests of drawers black sprigs were painted, to give the illusion of inlay. Other pieces of furniture which might have graced the homes of the more prosperous settlers were heavy court cupboards, writing boxes, and chairs of the stick- and ladder-back type. Many of the stick-back chairs were

BELOW *A chest of drawers, of oak and decorated with carved and painted designs, which was made in Ipswich, Massachusetts. It may have been ordered to commemmorate the marriage of John and Margaret Staniford in 1678.*

modelled upon one made for the prominent Puritan leader, Elder Brewster of Massachusetts, after whom they were named. Made of turned uprights, with double tiers of baluster-turned spindles on the back and sides, the Brewster chair was a fine example of the turner's craft. Similar, but lighter, was the Carver chair, so named after Governor Carver of the Massachusetts Bay Colony. Nearly all the furniture which is still in existence from this time shows very clearly that although the mother country provided the inspiration and pattern for fashions and

tastes in New England, individual regional characteristics, which can be seen as peculiarly American, were already developing.

The houses of the Dutch in New Amsterdam remained more traditional, and tended to be better equipped and more comfortably furnished than the houses of the English settlers. Traditional pieces to be found in the average Dutch home were caned stools and chairs, leather-upholstered chairs (sometimes), and especially the massive two-doored 'kas' or linen cupboards. 'Kas' were often gaily painted with colourful floral patterns, or *en grisaille*, in grey monochrome. After the English took over New Amsterdam in 1664 and made it New York, furniture modelled on these traditional Dutch pieces found its way into many English houses, both there and in other colonies.

Although there was no guild system in America, steps were taken fairly early on to ensure that certain standards would be maintained within the furniture industry. In Boston, which was culturally relatively advanced, the training policy for apprentices was systematized in 1660. A minimum of seven years (instead of the customary three or four years) was stipulated as being the necessary length of an indentureship. Apprenticeship usually began when a youth was about fourteen years old, and lasted until he was twenty-one, at which age he was considered responsible enough and sufficiently trained to set up his own business. But except in those cases where the newly qualified furniture-makers enjoyed financial backing, few could afford to establish their own practices immediately upon qualifying. It was common for them to travel around the country as journeymen, working for established furniture-makers for very meagre wages, but acquiring experience, and perhaps saving enough money as they went to eventually enable them to set up their own workshops.

The increasing wealth of the colonies along the eastern seaboard after the turn of the century inevitably brought with it increasing desire for comfort and luxury. More settlers were arriving all the time, with fresh inspiration from the countries of the Old World, particularly England, and bringing fresh talent as well. The William and Mary style was introduced into the colonies during the early years of the eighteenth century. Basically, this signified the introduction of a more architectural approach to furniture. Philadelphia, which had by now become the most prosperous city in America, led the way in furniture design, though Boston and Newport were also important centres. Chests of drawers were the most striking examples of the new style. There were several variations on the basic shape. A chest of drawers might be raised on a stand, with graceful turned legs, bowed skirting, and bun feet. Or sometimes, the basic chest of drawers had an additional section with a fall front, becoming a secretary desk (or bureau, which is the English word), like the stately one made by Edward Evans in Philadelphia in 1707 (the earliest extant signed and dated

piece from that city). Sometimes, the basic chest of drawers was surmounted by a bookcase, again with a fall front, making it a secretary desk-cum-bookcase. Gate-legged tables, modelled upon those familiar in England in the seventeenth century, were also introduced at this time. The American version of this table with turned supports was lighter than the English model. The butterfly table, first made in Connecticut, was an innovation based on this form. Its legs slanted slightly away from the top, and the supports for its hinged leaves were gracefully curved like butterfly wings.

In Philadelphia, as in England, the most popular wood was walnut. But there was a great variety of woods available for use in America, including maple, pine (both much used in New England), sycamore and fruit-woods, and these woods used in combination added variety and texture to colonial furniture. Contrasting woods were much in favour, as was 'jappaning', a technique imported from England and developed mainly in Boston. Where previously, in the seventeenth century, furniture had tended to be simple in its conception, but almost ornate at times in its decoration, furniture of the William and Mary period in America was elegant in conception, and often starkly simple in decoration. The dignified Philadelphia cabinets and the clear-lined butterfly tables are cases in point.

By the early 1720s, the graceful Queen Anne style was beginning to reach America. The most distinctive characteristic of this style was the cabriole leg. The gently curving 'S' shape began to appear on legs of cabinets, chairs, tables, and indeed on almost every kind of furniture. Harmonious curves were also used on chair backs and seat rails, and did much to lighten the heavier tone of the earlier William and Mary style. This new lightness was particularly apparent on pieces such as the chest on stand, or 'highboy', as it came to be called in the nineteenth century. The earlier form of heavy underframing strengthened with stretchers was replaced by a much more delicate form of construction using the curvaceous cabriole leg. Such elegance was matched with an increasing concern for comfort in seat furniture. The big upholstered wing chair, first made in New Hampshire, was one of the most luxurious pieces made in the colonies, and was soon to be found in all the most elegant houses of the towns dotting the eastern seaboard. Other new forms of furniture introduced during this period were the New England tea-tables and card-tables (symbols of the increasing availability of leisure time), both of which had, of course, cabriole legs, generally ending in pad feet. Upholstered settees and sofas joined wing chairs in the houses of the rich, and wooden chairs, flat in appearance, linear and gracefully curving in New England, more carved and plastic in Philadelphia, replaced the sterner, squarer chairs of the earlier part of the century. The continually improving shipping links between America and England during the course of the century inevitably led to some overlap of one style with another. Thus, for instance, a cabinet might, in general form, be a William and Mary piece, while some of its details might be categorized as Queen Anne. Or again, some pieces which were considered to be Queen Anne were, in fact, Georgian, as they showed marked Palladian influence. This fluidity of styles was especially noticeable in Philadelphia, since Philadelphia was the city closest to London in taste and fashions. An especially striking example of Palladian 'Queen Anne' furniture was the extraordinary cabinet for an air pump, made by John Harrison of Philadelphia in 1739. This cabinet has the form of a doorway, with Doric pilasters bordering the door, and a splendid broken pediment.

By the early 1760s, the graceful elegance of Queen Anne furniture began to give way to the freer, more ornate forms of the Rococo, the style which was given its impetus by the arrival in the colonies of Chippendale's *The Gentleman and Cabinet-Maker's Director*.

RIGHT   The magnificence of the staircase vault at the Würzburg Residenz—it is 105 feet in length and 60 feet wide—served to reflect the ambitions of the Prince of Würzburg. The staircase was designed by J. Balthasar Neumann and the grandiose ceiling decoration, depicting the four continents paying homage to the prince, was painted by the outstanding Venetian painter G. B. Tiepolo.

BELOW   An exuberantly carved and gilded seventeenth-century side table, designed for 'The Room of the Heroic Women' in La Rocca, palace of Prince Giampaolo Maria de Soragna. The top is covered with rich velvet and the legs are sculptured in the forms of scrolls and interlacing acanthus leaves, one of the most popular motifs of Baroque decoration.

FAR RIGHT   Carved and gilded side tables were generally made in sets to be accompanied by a pair of candlestands which were placed on either side of the table. Generally a wall-glass hung above the table to complete the set. The decoration on these items was matched, and before the sumptuary edicts of Louis XIV in 1689 many of them were made in silver. The architectural outlines of the table reflect Le Brun's influence, and it was not until after his death that scrolling forms were seen in France again.

LEFT A gilt side chair from a set made for Sir William Humphreys after he became Lord Mayor of London. It probably dates from 1717 when he was granted his own arms which are carved on the cresting. The present upholstery is modern; a luxuriously patterned cut velvet from Genoa would probably have been its original covering. This is an early example of a piece of furniture entirely decorated with gilt gesso, a technique which became popular during the Palladian period. Although the technique of gilding had been known since the Middle Ages, the gilding used at this time was of the highest quality ever achieved in England.

RIGHT A grand gilded wall-mirror designed in the architectural style of the Palladian movement. The female mask set against a background of acanthus leaves is typically Palladian, although the asymmetrical design of the cartouche placed between the curving forms of the broken pediment is thoroughly Rococo in conception. Like many fine eighteenth-century mirrors, this example was probably made in Ireland by the Booker family of Dublin.

BELOW A side table vigorously carved with winged female supports, scrolls, acanthus leaves and a magnificent satyr's head centring on the crossed stretchers. The grandeur of conception and execution illustrate the late seventeenth-century Baroque inspiration for this piece, now in the Palazzo Doria-Pamphili.

The Rococo Period

FROM THE TIME OF THE Renaissance, artists and architects in Europe had relied on the principles and guidelines of classical art for inspiration. But in the early eighteenth century, for the first time since the Renaissance, a style developed which was not inspired by the tenets of classicism. This new style, dominant in Europe during the first half of the eighteenth century, came to be known as Rococo. The term 'rococo' was first used in the middle of that century simply to describe the qualities of the art form which was prevalent at the time. The description in fact singled out only one aspect—rockwork—to describe the whole genre. Later in the century, students of the Neoclassical painter David used the term 'rococo' in a derogatory way, to signify their scorn for an art form which they considered frivolous, insubstantial, and luxurious to the point of decadence.

Though many of Rococo's basic forms derived from the Baroque style, Rococo as an art form arose as a rejection of the formal grandeur of Baroque. The architect-designers working for the French aristocracy and court used delicate curvilinear shapes like 'C' and 'S' scrolls, placing them asymmetrically, as if to agitate the overall dynamism of a design. Natural forms of flowers, bushes and trees were abundant, and rockwork and shellwork were incorporated to give an even more vivid sense of 'nature'. In its exaggerated grace and ornamentation, furniture became more and more frivolous. Exoticism was another element of Rococo furniture, and oriental motifs became popular, particularly in the work of English furniture-makers.

Baroque art, in its formal, symmetrical grandeur, promoted and glorified the power of the great—in France, of the monarch. But the hierarchical formality of court life in France gradually began to be relaxed, and by the time of Louis XIV's death, the aristocratic way of life had already changed considerably. Gaiety, luxury, intimacy and freedom from restraints were the new aristocratic ideals, and in France was evolved the style that expressed and embodied those ideals. The magnificent and

RIGHT *Despite indications in the second half of the eighteenth century that the state apartments were on the decline, they continued to be necessary additions to elegant houses and were decorated in the most sumptuous way. This state bedchamber at Nostell Priory was the work of the fashionable Rococo architect-designer, James Paine, whose designs for the ceiling show a marked affinity with contemporary French examples. The chimney piece, however, despite its Rococo ornamentation, is in the more conservative Palladian style. The furniture in this room, which included a set of 'India armchairs' at 2½ guineas each, a green japanned commode and a pier glass, as well as a state bed, was supplied by Thomas Chippendale, whose firm was also responsible for hanging the imported, hand-painted wallpaper in 1771.*

awe-inspiring marble halls, galleries and presence chambers of the Baroque court were divided up and converted into smaller rooms. Intimate reception rooms, in the forms of drawing rooms and boudoirs, were decorated with lighter colours than before, and an enormous range of light and feminine furniture was there distributed in studied informality. Behind the grand and sombre apartments of Louis XIV at Versailles, Louis XV, who 'thought of himself not as a king, but as the richest and most gorgeous noble in the kingdom' (Maillard), had his own charming *petits appartements*, which he actually used.

In the more formal courts of Germany, and in Italy, where many princes continued to promulgate late seventeenth-century Baroque ideals of courtly splendour, the Rococo style was appropriated as a magnificent decorative device, to be superimposed on basically Baroque forms. Thus in France and Germany, Rococo was used to achieve different ends—in France, to create comfort and to bring about a sense of intimacy, and in Germany to embellish the grandeur of princely interiors.

The eighteenth century saw the rise of an ever-growing middle class in both Europe and America, which was brought about by an unprecedented increase in commercial activity everywhere. The *nouveaux riches* in both Europe and America were quick to adopt the fashions hitherto available only to a few aristocrats, and were soon furnishing their houses in the Rococo style. This trend was immensely helped by the publication of many books of furniture design, notably Chippendale's *The Gentleman and Cabinet-Maker's Director*.

Rococo by its very nature was destined to be short-lived, for it was a purely decorative art form, light and insubstantial. By the early 1760s, the pure forms of Neoclassicism were already replacing the brilliantly capricious forms of Rococo, and in the spirit of pre-revolutionary Republicanism in France, Rococo came to be regarded as a symbol of the immorality and hedonism of the *ancien régime*.

France

In 1715, old King Louis XIV died, and with him went the last vestiges of the cold, grand and formal style which he had espoused during his long reign. His successor was his great-grandson, Louis XV, a child of five, so a Regent was appointed to govern the affairs of state during the young king's minority. This was the Duc d'Orléans, a witty, artistic, pleasure-loving man. Although he effectively ruled for only eight years, from 1715 to 1723, the force of his personality left its mark on French society. The artistic period now called the Régence is generally regarded as extending from 1700 to 1730, and can be seen as the first phase of the Rococo style in France.

RIGHT *A handsome cupboard, probably made around 1725, decorated with gilt bronze mounts and veneered in purplewood in radiating geometric patterns. Elaborate wardrobes were not as fashionable as commodes in the eighteenth century, but this fine example is attributed to the ébéniste Charles Cressent, who specialized in modelling very fine bronze mounts which he applied to his furniture.*

LEFT *This intimately observed domestic scene of a family at breakfast ('Le Petit Dejeuner' by François Boucher) shows how adaptable Rococo furniture was to an informal way of life.*

During the opening years of the eighteenth century, France was faced with economic recession and political and social unrest, due in part to the failure of Louis XIV's disastrous war policies. Tired of the austerity of Versailles, much of the court began to take up residence in Paris, and the Duc d'Orléans established his own brilliant court at his family seat, the Palais Royale. Innumerable town houses were built, and architects and decorators refashioned the interiors of many others to reflect the new tastes and changing milieu in which eighteenth-century French society found itself. From the beginning of the Régence, Paris became the centre of a highly sophisticated, cosmopolitan society which admitted financiers and intellectuals, drawn from the *nouveaux riches*, into the old orders of the established aristocracy. Women too, played an increasingly important role in society, presiding over intimate gatherings where the arts of conversation, charm, and wit were highly valued. This was a trend which continued throughout the period. One of the most notable women of the period was Madame de Pompadour, the brilliantly cultured mistress of Louis XV, whose own artistic tastes were widely reflected in the arts. It was only natural that the increasing demands for intimacy should be reflected in interior design and especially in furniture.

As early as 1690, the year of Le Brun's death, there had been a perceptible change in decorative styles. The heavy, classicized splendour of Le Brun's style, so vigorously fostered by designers like Jean Le Pautre, had given way to the lighter surface decoration favoured by Le Pautre's son, Pierre, and by Jean Bérain. Although not free from the restraints of symmetry, the arabesques and lambrequins (scalloped materials) of Bérain's designs showed a greater freedom of movement than had been seen hitherto. But it was Le Pautre who took the initiative to transpose Bérain's two-dimensional style of decoration into a three-dimensional style. This was particularly noticeable in wall panels, where surface sculptural decoration overran the panel frames and trickled into the surrounding space beyond, thus breaking with the architectural and functional articulation of the wall and allowing the surface ornamentation to emerge as the dominant feature. This new type of decoration was a complete departure from the tradition of the preceding century, with its grand columns framing monumental painted wall decorations, and it was not

BELOW LEFT *A delightful* bureau de dame *by C. Wolff. The interior is fitted with a series of small drawers and pigeonholes. Such a feminine piece could only have been made for a lady such as Madame de Pompadour, to whom it was delivered in about 1755.*

BELOW RIGHT *A small, elegant table, typical of the feminine pieces of furniture which were suited to the intimate interiors of the Rococo period. The lozenge-shaped pattern on the legs is painted in* vernis Martin *(lacquer) and was designed to match the Sèvres porcelain top, although it has yellowed with age.*

LEFT *This commode à vantaux differs from an ordinary commode only in that the drawers are concealed by two cupboard doors, a style followed in the best English examples of the 1770s. It was made by Pierre Migeon II, a favourite cabinet-maker of Madame de Pompadour. The polychrome marquetry includes woods such as tulipwood and purplewood, and the sinuous outline is subtly emphasized by a darker coloured wood and protective gilt bronze mounts.*

BELOW *A luxurious and comfortable type of chaise longue, known as a veilleuse. Designed for a lady to recline on, it is one of a wide variety of the lounging seat furniture popular during Louis XV's reign. It was frequently placed so as to face another veilleuse.*

RIGHT *The* voyeuse *is a variation of the* bergère *type of armchair introduced during the Régence (1715–23). Beech was a wood frequently employed by the* menuisiers *for seat furniture, and this example has the luxurious addition of gilding. Comfort became an important consideration in chair-making during the eighteenth century. The padded back rail provided support for a participant in a conversation.*

long before furniture too was designed to harmonize with this lighter, more frivolous type of interior scheme. The strict rules of etiquette which had governed the use and deployment of furniture, notably chairs, under the old régime of Louis XIV were disregarded. Chairs were no longer required to stand in rigid conformation along the sides of walls. Even their forms were modified. It was during this period that the *bergère*, the original comfortable, upholstered armchair, came into being. A softer curvilinear outline replaced the austerity of the rectilinear design of the Baroque. Profiles took on undulating, serpentine and other curvilinear shapes; legs were generally elegantly curved with scrolled feet. The high-backed chair, so typical of the autocratic court of Louis XIV, was lowered so as not to interfere with the elegant coiffures of the women, and the arms were set back to allow for the voluminous folds of fabric covering their newly fashionable panniered skirts.

The two most notable figures of the Régence were the architect G. M. Oppenordt and the *ébéniste* Charles Cressent. Oppenordt, the son of a Dutch cabinet-maker, was the architect-designer most associated with the period, and was responsible for decorating the Duc d'Orléans' Palais

ABOVE *A commode by Charles Cressent, the favourite ébéniste of the Regent, the Duc d'Orléans. The double curve and bombé form of this complex piece was described as en arc d'arbalette (cross-bow-shaped) by Cressent. The lavish bronze mounts in the form of Rococo sprays and scrolls, cartouches and winged dragons centre on a single head, a device popularized by the painter Watteau. The fiery dragons are cunningly devised to form the drawer handles, as shown in the detail, right.*

Royale in the new fashion. Cressent was probably the finest furniture-maker in the early Rococo style. His furniture met the requirements of the times, its lightness superseding the heavier, more sombre furniture produced in the workshops of André-Charles Boulle during the last years of the old king's reign. Cressent's lighter touch, his more fluent way with opulence, is especially well illustrated by his innovative commode, which dates from about 1730. The commode itself had been an important innovation in the early years of the eighteenth century and continued to be one of the most lavishly decorated items throughout both Louis XV's and his successor's reigns. The gilt bronze head was a decorative device popularized by Watteau, although the architect Robert de Cotte was known to have used the motif to decorate the chapel doors at Versailles as early as 1710. The commode of the late Régence illustrates the fluent use of the new curvilinear forms and the vigour and animation in its bronze mounts is thoroughly Rococo in conception. Cressent had been trained as a sculptor, and his wonderfully sculpted bronze accessories

brought him into conflict with the rigorous Paris guilds. The members of the guilds jealously protected their own interests and forbade the employment of two such distinctly separate crafts as sculpture and *ébénisterie* within a single workshop. But Cressent won the day, and soon bronze accessories became the necessary additions on all veneered, lacquered or marquetried furniture of quality. There were several bronze workers of considerable note, among whom was Philippe Caffieri (1714–74) who, like his father and grandfather before him, enjoyed a reputation in his own day which placed him on a par with that of the most eminent *ébénistes*.

But, generally, early examples of Rococo lacked the dynamism of the true Louis XV style which made its appearance in the third decade of the century. It was the age of Louis XV which saw the full flowering of the Rococo style in France. The innovations of the Régence contributed to the Rococo period, and Régence ideas were further extended to create a fresh style which, through the sheer scope of its fantasy, captured the

ABOVE *Elaborately carved and gilded console tables were still the work of the* menuisiers *during the eighteenth century despite the preponderance of* ébénistes. *Claude Roumier was the principal carver working for the French crown in the middle of the century, and this piece was sculpted by him for the Palace of Versailles. Console tables, often the finest examples of the* menuisier's *skills, continued to be important and decorative items of furniture in the eighteenth century.*

ABOVE *A bed* à la polonaise, *made by the menuisier Nicholas Heurtant (1720–71) in the Rococo style. The name was particularly appropriate at this time as the wife of Louis XV was born a Polish princess.*

LEFT *A looking glass in the Régence style fashionable from 1715 to 1723 when the infant Louix XV's uncle, the Duc d'Orléans, acted as Regent of France. This transitional piece has both Baroque and Rococo elements, though it lacks the sombre formality of the former and the refinement of the later style.*

imagination of Europe. Except in architecture which, in France at least, continued to be influenced by classicism, the Rococo represented the antithesis of the classical art form which had had its first impulses in antiquity and which, under various guises, had continued to dominate European art since the Renaissance.

The prime innovators of the Rococo style during the Louis XV period, which lasted from approximately 1730 to 1760, were the designers Juste Aurèle Meissonnier (1695–1750) and Nicholas Pineau (1684–1754). Meissonnier, although a native of France, had been born and brought up in the Italian city of Turin, a city in which the forms and concepts of late seventeenth-century Baroque tastes prevailed. It was here that he trained and worked for a while before returning, in 1726, to Paris where he was appointed *Dessinateur de la Chambre et du Cabinet du Roi*, succeeding Jean Bérain who died the same year. In this important position, Meissonnier had a tremendous influence, not only in France, but throughout Europe; indeed, Paris was the first city to tire of his outrageous compositions. It was he who, through his engraved designs, popularized the

ABOVE LEFT *A corner cabinet, or* encoignure, *made by G. Joubert. The large areas of purplewood geometric marquetry, or parquetry, decorated with gilded bronze mounts in the rocaille taste were particularly fashionable during the second quarter of the eighteenth century.*

ABOVE RIGHT *A detail of the corner cabinet above left showing the gilded bronze medallion on the front. The medallion features allegorical figures within a rocaille frame surrounded by garlands of flowers and foliage and coins.*

rocaille (rockwork) ornamentation, which was to become one of the central elements of the Rococo style for the next thirty years. The profusion of rockwork, lightheartedly combined with carved cascading waterfalls, foliage and scallop shells, was known as the *genre pittoresque*. The forms became more and more exaggerated, eventually spiralling into whorls and distorted curls and curves which unleashed a degree of animation not hitherto imagined. Asymmetrical scrolls were added, further evoking the sense of restlessness and continuous movement already inherent in Rococo. The works of Meissonnier were occasionally likened to the perpetual motion of waves.

Nicholas Pineau's work was more restrained than Meissonnier's, and his designs for furniture had a more lasting influence on French Rococo decoration. Pineau returned from Russia to Paris in 1727 and was promptly acclaimed the leader of the new style. His drawings and designs, many of which have been preserved in the engravings of Mariette, display a delicacy and grace not seen in Meissonnier's work. He provided designs for the interiors of many Parisian houses, including the Hôtel du Mazarin. The rooms in these houses, with their gold and white *boiseries*, or wall panels, were much smaller than the grand salons of Louis XIV's court. The tendency was to replace the grand sequences of state rooms with smaller, more intimate rooms, such as those which were designed for Louis XV at Versailles. Rooms were often only ten or twelve feet high, and furniture was usually made to scale. Furniture was frequently designed as an integral part of the overall scheme, with motifs being picked up as much on the *boiseries* as on the furniture itself. One of the most widely used motifs during the Rococo period was that of a flower entwined with lightly scrolling curves.

The preference for lighter, gayer colours extended not only to the wall decorations but also to furniture. The dark, sombre woods used previously by *ébénistes* such as Boulle were replaced by new woods from the East and West Indies, woods with exotic sounding names such as *palisandre*, *bois de rose* and *bois de violette*. *Bois de rose*, which had a striking purple colour, was much coveted by *ébénistes* for marquetry and veneering. In a description of furniture-making techniques of the day, the *maître menuisier* André Jacob Roubo named no less than fifty different types of wood which could be used to create brilliant and subtle contrasts in colour and tone. But, unfortunately, the brilliance and polychromatic effects achieved during the eighteenth century have been largely lost, due to the effects of handling and exposure to air.

During the years of the Régence, a geometric style of marquetry had been dominant on much furniture. Gilt bronze mounts, trailing over the pieces, lent the otherwise slightly heavy forms some animation and frivolity. Towards the end of the Régence period, mounts were used

ABOVE *This fine* secrétaire à abattant *was made by J.-F. Dubut. Its small size and graceful lines suggest that it was intended for use by a lady. The lacquer panels incorporated into the front of the piece were imported from the orient and contribute to the luxurious appearance of this delightful Rococo piece.*

less, and a new type of marquetry, depicting sprays of flowers, emerged. At the same time, furniture became generally lighter in form. Later, during the transitional period of the 1760s, marquetry became more and more complex, and delightful pictorial designs replaced the earlier geometric patterns.

Among the finest marqueteurs of the eighteenth century was a man whose name was for long unknown. His work could be recognized only by the initials B. V. R. B. Not until 1957 was B. V. R. B. identified as the *maître ébéniste* Bernard Van Risamburgh. Like many other cabinet-makers of the day, Van Risamburgh was employed by eminent Parisian dealers (such as the famous Duvaux), who acted as middlemen in their dealings between the cabinet-maker and his royal or aristocratic patrons. It seems that a deliberate policy of secrecy led the *marchands-merciers* to conceal the names and identities of these brilliant furniture-makers.

Lacquered furniture, whether imported from the East or made in France, was wildly fashionable in France, as elsewhere in Europe. Cabinet-makers such as Criard, Dubois and Van Risamburgh excelled at making this type of furniture. Imported lacquered panels, removed from their

LEFT *A magnificent* grande commode *made for the Cabinet du Roi at Versailles. Made by Antoine Gaudreau in the style of the Slodtz brothers, it was designed and made in 1729 for Louis XV to house his coin collection. The gilded bronze mounts may have been made by the Slodtz brothers themselves or by Caffieri.*

BELOW LEFT *A small* encoignure, *the work of Bernard Van Risamburgh, which was recognized by his initials B.V.R.B. Like a few other furniture-makers, Van Risamburgh worked for one of the well-known dealers, or marchands-merciers, who were responsible for selling the pieces to patrons. His pieces are distinguished by the thin ormulu frames and borders.*

screens, were skilfully incorporated into the curved surfaces of commodes and writing tables. Imitation lacquer, or *vernis*, which was developed by the Martin brothers, became so popular that it was given the name *vernis Martin.*

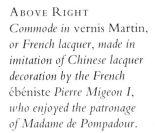

ABOVE RIGHT *Commode in* vernis Martin, *or French lacquer, made in imitation of Chinese lacquer decoration by the French ébéniste Pierre Migeon I, who enjoyed the patronage of Madame de Pompadour.*

BELOW RIGHT *A magnificent commode by Bernard Van Risamburgh, lacquered in the technique perfected by the four Martin brothers and since known as* vernis Martin. *The carcass of this commode is partly of oak and partly of pine, and the lacquer panels on the front two drawers are treated as a single piece, thus maintaining the pictorial unity of the design.*

The importance of women in society had a far-reaching effect on furniture design generally. In many respects, the form of much furniture was essentially feminine. Even the terms used to describe many items of furniture reflected this: the *siège à la reine*, a flat-backed chair without arms; the *marquise*, an intimate sofa, wider and deeper than the *bergère*; the *ottomane* with its graceful curving ends; and the *duchesse*, which had a back at one end and an extended seat. Like nearly all carved furniture of the period, most seat furniture was decorated with the fluid curving outlines so typical of the Rococo period. The cabriole leg, the curved back (wittily described as '*en cabriolet*' by Louis XV), and the frames were carved with delicate posies of flowers and other Rococo motifs. Made by *menuisiers* and carvers, these chairs satisfied society's demands for luxury and personal comfort. In keeping with the structural quality, upholstery too was more delicate. Lightly coloured silks and brocades were used, and heavier velvets were generally in pale pastel colours. Towards the middle of the eighteenth century, commodes became smaller. As in the case of seat furniture, there were several new variations

ABOVE *A caned walnut sofa, or* canapé, *by the provincial furniture-maker Pierre Nogaret. Although originally from Paris he preferred to work in Lyons, and many of his pieces are stamped 'Nogaret à Lyons'. His work is very similar to that of contemporary Parisian furniture-makers, as his confident handling of the Rococo outline shows. A cushion was used to add comfort to the seat of this sofa, which was made as part of a larger drawing-room suite, probably around 1750.*

ABOVE *A combined writing and toilet table, probably executed by the German-born cabinet-maker Jean-François Oeben.*

on the basic commode, such as the triangular *encoignures* or corner cupboards, which were usually made in matched pairs. Beds were elaborately draped and upholstered, and they too became lighter in appearance; paler-coloured textiles contributed to this effect. During the course of Louis XV's reign, the use of terms such as *lit à la polonaise* and

ABOVE *This magnificent* bureau à cylindre *is one of the most famous pieces to be made for Louis XV. Begun by the master* ébéniste *Jean-François Oeben, but unfinished at his death, it was completed by his even more famous assistant, Jean-Henri Riesener, who was responsible for the marquetry decoration. The roll-top device was invented by Oeben and quickly surpassed drop-front (*secrétaire*) and slant-top desks in popularity.*

à la turque to describe contemporary forms illustrates the fascination with the exotic prevalent at the time.

Different types of tables proliferated, each with a specific function. Console tables, lighter and more delicate than they had been in the previous century, were still the province of the *menuisier*, and were superbly carved with a profusion of delicate rocaille ornament. The *bonheur du jour* was intended to hold writing materials, and a wide range of dainty tables was made, such as the *coiffeuse* (to hold hairdressing items like wigs and hair-pins), and the *poudreuse* (to hold beauty patches). There were various exquisitely made gaming tables, and *chiffonières* for sewing equipment. Smaller items such as these could easily be moved about the room.

Few items were made on a large or 'masculine' scale, although one of the most famous pieces extant–the monumental roll-top *bureau du roi*– is an exception. Made for the king by one of the finest *ébénistes* of the eighteenth century, J. F. Oeben (1720–63), it was uncompleted at Oeben's death. Another notable *ébéniste* of German origin, J. H. Riesener, was responsible for completing this superb piece, but by the time it was finished, Rococo was no longer in fashion. It had been replaced by Neoclassicism, the form which was to dominate artistic direction in France for the rest of the century.

England

Rococo had been established in France since the beginning of the eighteenth century, but not until the 1730s was there any intimation that it might become fashionable in England. The sober Englishman was not inclined to embrace Rococo forms with the same ease and joy as his pleasure-loving French counterpart. This was partly due to the fact that Rococo in England followed hard upon the Palladian movement, whereas in France, Rococo more logically followed the Baroque period. Although Baroque furniture had in fact been popular throughout the Palladian period in England, the Palladian ideal was anti-Baroque, and the gap between Palladian severity and Rococo frivolity was a difficult one to bridge. Rococo in England, even at its height, was a decorative style, rather than an architectural form in its own right, and its pre-eminence

BELOW   *A massive, finely figured and carved dressing and writing table designed as one of a pair, the parts of which, when placed back to back, formed a centre library table. The profusion of the ormolu work and the heavy curvilinear design of the piece recall German work; it is attributed to the workshop of John Channon in St Martin's Lane. Channon was noted for his brass inlaid and decorated furniture.*

as a style only lasted for about twenty years before it was superseded by Neoclassicism.

One of the earliest commissions in the new Rococo style was given by the Duke of Kingston to the great French designer, Juste Aurèle Meissonnier, in 1735. It was for a suite of table furniture, which included tureens and a magnificent centre-piece to be executed in silver. Indeed, goldsmiths and silversmiths, particularly those of Huguenot descent, who were especially receptive to French tastes, led the way in developing Rococo in England. The purely decorative forms of the Rococo were easily adapted to meet their requirements. Other designers and craftsmen also realized the variable potential of the charming and delicate Rococo forms. Rococo embellished the borders of tradesmen's cards, billheads and bookplates before it began to be adapted to suit the demands of the furniture-makers. But it was not until around 1740 that the florid Baroque formality of William Kent's furniture designs finally gave way to the lighter, more delicate forms of the Rococo.

The new style of Rococo was in complete contrast to the severe Classicism of the Palladian school. The architectural frames, which had been used extensively for Palladian interiors and furniture designs, were replaced by the delicate scrolling shapes of Rococo. Architectural pediments and columns gave way to the shells and rocks of 'French' rocaille and to shallow, curling 'C' forms. The vitality which this shape exuded

ABOVE *French influence on English furniture led to the introduction of commodes into Britain from the 1730s onwards. By the middle of the century they were regarded as essential pieces of furniture, to be displayed in the most important reception rooms. They are usually elaborately decorated and this japanned example is unusual in having pierced lattice doors at either side. It was part of the set belonging to the Chinese Bedroom from Badminton House, Gloucestershire.*

was harnessed in an extraordinary number of different ways to provide an enormous range of effects. The outer rims of mirrors, testers and chimney-pieces took on sinuous, delicate curves, or became dramatic flamelike borders throwing off spiky projections into the air. The use of 'S' and serpentine shapes was a natural extension of the simpler 'C' form, and the play of asymmetrically placed forms was to become a hallmark of the Rococo style in England.

At the same time that French Rococo was being modified in England, Chinese decoration came into vogue. There was also a revival of the 'Gothick' style, which was concerned solely with the fantastic and picturesque. Chinoiserie and Gothick styles introduced a wide range of motifs and ornaments to an already highly imaginative repertoire. Another aspect of the Rococo style in England was the frequent portrayal of pastoral scenes. The addition of people to landscapes added charm to the more abstract exuberance of French Rococo designs and were natural extensions of the motifs of chinoiserie designs.

There was a large number of pattern books published during the middle of the century. Initially, furniture designs had been incorporated into pattern books produced by architects, artists and builders rather than by craftsmen, but gradually, furniture craftsmen came to appreciate the great possibilities of producing their own designs primarily for the use of other furniture-making workshops, but also for patrons with whom

these workshops often had close ties. One of the earliest publications in the new style was a book of patterns by Gaetano Brunetti, published in 1736, but his designs are hampered by a heaviness which indicates that he lacked a proper understanding of the Rococo form still emerging in England at this date. *The Gentleman's or Builder's Companion* by William Jones, published in 1739, presented some of the first designs to advertise the new fashion of Rococo. In it were included designs pirated from the French Rococo designer Nicholas Pineau, whose light, fanciful compositions were well received in England. Among the most popular designs were those for console tables, decorated with playful designs along the legs and friezes, and with fine marble tops. A Frenchman working in England, de la Cour, also published a number of designs between the years of 1741 and 1746, notably a series of chair patterns incorporating a form of interlacing bands. These patterns, similar to

ABOVE LEFT *Although this chair is of solid mahogany, it is decorated with a crossgrain veneer of mahogany, which is set at right angles to emphasize the interlacing figure-of-eight pattern of the back.*

ABOVE RIGHT *A superb solid mahogany armchair. The break with the ponderous appearance of the Palladian style is fully accomplished in this elegant piece.*

ABOVE *Elaborate commodes such as this are rare in Britain. The quality of the carving is exceptional and it is similar to a design in the* Director. *Its rather heavy appearance makes it seem very coarse in comparison to lighter, more refined French examples. Like many English commodes, it has three drawers, the handles of which are shown above right, as opposed to contemporary French pieces which generally have two.*

figures of eight, were widely used by chair-makers and designers, like Matthew Darly and Robert Mainwaring.

In 1744 a famous carver and designer, Mathias Lock (active 1740–69), published his very important designs for 'six sconces', followed two years later by his designs for 'six tables'. Both publications were of seminal importance for the development of English Rococo. The designs show the strength of the French influence on Lock; but more important, they display his own lightness of touch, and his understanding of the relationship between Rococo form and ornament. Previously in England a semblance of the Rococo style had been achieved by applying Rococo motifs to rather cumbersome structures retained from times past. Lock synthesized ornament and form into highly imaginative and coherent compositions, which were later augmented by designers of the calibre of Thomas Johnson and Thomas Chippendale. Unfortunately, few pieces produced in Lock's workshop remain.

The fact that few furniture-makers identified their handiwork has presented a considerable problem to historians of furniture. Unlike their French counterparts, English furniture-makers were not controlled by guild regulations and in many instances only bills of sale or correspondence between client and workshop proprietor has enabled accurate identification to take place.

The Rococo designs of the middle of the eighteenth century had a strong appeal to carvers, since Rococo forms made full use of their very considerable skills. Like the stuccoists and interior decorators, carvers indulged in a freedom of interpretation and imagination rarely seen in furniture-making. Pieces of furniture became fantastic works of the carver's art, masterpieces in their own right. In the case of mirrors,

girandoles (wall lights) and chimney pieces, the carvers hardly appeared to be hampered at all by functional considerations. Mahogany, imported from Cuba and Honduras, was a perfect foil for the cutters' tools. The clear, crisp lines which could be achieved on it made mahogany the most widely sought-after timber by the middle of the century. Other woods which might be expected to be found in the timber stocks of a cabinet-maker's yard would be oak, rosewood and perhaps padouk. Softer woods, notably pine, deal and beech would be used in making the carcasses for veneering, japanning or gilding. Japanning was a technique used by several furniture-makers, the best known of whom was the joiner Giles Grendy. The softer materials were easier to cut, so the carver could achieve sinuous agile lines which could then be covered with a brilliant layer of gilding. Gilding was still used for the most important pieces, especially console tables, girandoles and mirror frames, the most decorative pieces of the Rococo period.

The period 1750–60 was a decade of almost unparalleled productivity and inventiveness. The year 1754 was marked by the publication of the

ABOVE *Small breakfast tables had been referred to in inventories since Tudor times, but there was a marked increase in their popularity in the eighteenth century. This was probably because of the late hours of rising kept by members of fashionable society. The design of the table is identical to one in Chippendale's* Director, *in which 'the front is cut out for a recess for the knees'. Although on this piece the fret-work sides are of carved wood, delicate wire grilles were used to protect the contents in the interior of the cupboard.*

most important book of Rococo furniture design: Thomas Chippendale's great pattern book *The Gentleman and Cabinet-Maker's Director*. Chippendale's *Director* was the first pattern book devoted entirely to furniture designs, and in it Chippendale incorporated patterns for every conceivable type of furniture, including designs in Chinese and Gothick taste, as well as in French. Nearly all of the 160 engraved plates exhibit the light-hearted gaiety of the Rococo style. The ribband-back chair is the most identifiable of Chippendale's designs, although he may in fact have been influenced by French designs for this pattern. Chippendale gave ribband-back chairs their name, and said: '. . . if I may speak without vanity, they are the best I have ever seen.' This chair was the carver's delight, providing him a superb opportunity to demonstrate his abilities.

Although Chippendale never made a fortune, as other cabinet-makers are known to have done, it is clear that his workshop was both extensive

and fashionable. Like other leading cabinet-makers of the day, he employed a wide number of artists, designers and craftsmen.

The publication of the *Director* in 1754 generated several rival pattern books. In 1755 a hitherto unknown designer, Thomas Johnson, published his pattern books of designs for 'twelve girandoles'. Each girandole was designed to be carved from a soft wood, gessoed, and finally gilded. They are among the liveliest and most romantic of all Rococo designs, and feature characters drawn from *Aesop's Fables* (which Johnson knew from Francis Barlow's illustrations published in the previous century). More of Johnson's wonderfully delicate and extravagantly naturalistic designs for console tables, girandoles, mirror and picture frames and candlestands appeared in 1756 and 1757.

The English had been much interested in the orient since the previous century, but it was not until the middle of the eighteenth century that oriental art really flowered in England. The oriental style was readily assimilable into the forms and ornament of the Rococo. With the notable

ABOVE LEFT *This delicately carved and gilded wall-mirror is attributed to Thomas Johnson and is certainly modelled on a design in his publication of 1758,* One Hundred and Fifty New Designs. *It shows one of Johnson's favourite animals, the squirrel.*

ABOVE RIGHT *Detail of the Chinese Room at Claydon House, Buckinghamshire, showing the doorway. The interior was designed by Luke Lightfoot.*

ABOVE LEFT *A painted mirror of the type fashionable during the Rococo period.*

ABOVE RIGHT *Mahogany tea or china tables were essential for the tea ceremony which, by the eighteenth century, was a common occurrence in 'polite' society. On this tea table the etiolated cabriole legs and the delicately pierced fret-work gallery are* a tour de force *of contemporary carving.*

exception of William Chambers, the designers and furniture-makers of the day had not been anywhere near China, so the forms and motifs which became their stock-in-trade were often eccentric. They were taken from the themes and motifs found on the lacquer screens and oriental porcelain imported during the reign of Charles II, and from the decorative painted wall papers from China which were very popular bedroom decorations in the mid-eighteenth century. Dragons and mandarins moving among pagodas and temples were transposed to furniture. Then the painted pagodas were used as architectural blueprints, and chinoiserie was extended to the building of small pagodas and ornamental temples for outside use. They were frequently designed to accommodate the newly fashionable mode of tea-drinking, a pastime imported from the East which was fast becoming a habit. Among the best known of these pavilions was the pagoda designed by Chambers for the Royal Gardens at Kew in 1762. Chambers had, at the age of sixteen, travelled with the Swedish East India Company to China, where he had made extensive

notes and drawings, later published in folio form. He seems to have felt extremely defensive about his touring: 'I cannot conceive why it should be criminal in a traveller to give an account of what he has seen worthy of notice in China, any more than in Italy, France or any other country.' The folio covers an extensive range of subjects, including 'furniture, utensils, machines and dresses.' He goes on to say that 'those of the furniture were taken from such models as appeared to me the most beautiful and reasonable; some of them are pretty and may be useful to our cabinet-makers.' There is, however, no evidence to suggest that his illustrations of Chinese furniture, published in 1757, were copied in England, and his later academic training and subsequent preferences led him to conclude that he did not really wish 'to promote a taste so much inferior to the antique and so very unfit for our climate.'

Not surprisingly, japanning and imported lacquerwork were used for the new chinoiserie decoration and included items such as chairs, beds and commodes. Among the most exotic pieces of furniture was a magnificent bed designed *en suite* with a commode, chairs and hanging china shelves for the Duke of Beaufort. Rococo furniture, particularly 'in the Chinese taste', was very popular for decorating bedrooms which were lined with exquisite hand-painted wall papers imported from China. Designed as part of an overall furniture scheme, the Badminton House Chinese bedroom furniture was for long considered to be executed to a design by Thomas Chippendale, but recent research indicates that it was probably the work of his contemporary, John Linnell. The bed is in the form of an open-sided Chinese temple; the tester is dramatically shaped as a pagoda roof and embellished with lively spitting dragons which guard each corner. They are perched on the top of elegant 'C' shaped scrolls so typical of the Rococo, and spiky 'C' shaped flames pierce the air round the rim of the tester. The open latticework of the headboard is in the Chinese style and is a type of decoration widely used on all types of furniture including the doors of the commode which forms part of the suite.

Chippendale was noted for employing this type of pierced fretwork decoration on a number of pieces. The rather angular quality of the design lent itself in particular to chairs and he produced '9 designs of chairs after the Chinese manner.' The legs of much furniture in the style reverted to the square cut straight form and Chippendale added stretchers, more, it seems, for decorative effect than for any additional support.

For all its widespread popularity, chinoiserie had a number of critics who resented the fact that 'chairs, tables, chimney pieces, frames for looking glasses and even our most vulgar utensils are all reduced to this newfangled standard.' Chippendale himself, though he was particularly noted for his own use of chinoiserie, expressed reserve; it was, he said, a

NEAR RIGHT *A bed in the form of an Oriental pavilion or temple. Designed as part of the Chinese state bedroom furniture at Badminton House for the fourth Duke of Beaufort, the set includes commodes and chairs which, like the bed, are decorated in the Oriental manner, with red and green japanned decoration and pierced fret-work. The suite is attributed to William Linnell, whose workshop was at 28 Berkeley Square, London.*

FAR RIGHT *The Strawberry Room at Lee Priory takes its name from Horace Walpole's Gothick extravaganza Strawberry Hill. This small study was designed by James Wyatt in about 1785 in the Gothick style.*

style which had never yet 'arrived to any perfection . . . [but] admits the greatest variety'.

The revival of the Gothick style, which had never entirely disappeared in England, was another whimsical method of exploring the picturesque themes so fashionable for interior decorating schemes. But where the Gothick taste differed from both chinoiserie and the French Rococo styles was that, in England at least, its first reappearance was in architecture. Architects such as Hawksmoor, Vanbrugh and William Kent had trifled with it. Kent had published a volume of furniture designs in the Gothick style, but these designs in fact had merely applied the superficial ornaments of the style to articles designed along the solid guidelines of Palladian architecture. Batty Langley, who was a prolific writer and designer, tried his hand at the Gothick, but achieved results similar to Kent's as the title to his book illustrates: *Gothick Architecture Improved by Rules and Proportions, in many Grand Designs of Columns . . . Temples and Pavilions.*

Horace Walpole was regarded by many as the chief protagonist in the Gothick revival. He considered Langley a 'barbarous architect', and in the 1740s set out to transform his house, Strawberry Hill, into a real

Gothick masterpiece. Walpole was one of the first patrons in the eighteenth century to examine original Gothick decorations and to incorporate his findings into his building designs. He also incorporated Gothick motifs into the furniture and interiors of Strawberry Hill in preference to the prevailing French Rococo or chinoiserie tastes of the day. While his designs were solidly based on original Gothick designs, he did say that his villa was more the 'work of fancy than of imitation'. There were others who used the new Gothick forms, notably Sanderson Miller, who designed several buildings in the Gothick style, as well as the interior decorations for buildings such as Lacock Abbey in Wiltshire, and James Wyatt, who designed the Strawberry Room at Lee Priory.

The designs and motifs of Gothick were usually drawn from existing examples such as Archbishop Wareham's tomb in Canterbury Cathedral, and the fan vaulting of ceilings such as those found in St George's Chapel, Windsor, and Henry VII's chapel in Westminster Abbey, London. Among the designers of the day who used this style was Thomas Chippendale, who was so much at ease with all the prevailing fashions. The masculine severity of the style was well suited to library furniture and bachelor rooms. Bookcases were medievalized and decorated with arched doors, quatrefoils replaced latticework glazing bars, finials became pinnacles, and chairs became throne-like.

Of all the aspects of Rococo in England, Gothick was the most masculine. Its popularity was not so widespread as the popularity of French

Rococo and chinoiserie, but Gothick was to outlast the others. In fact, Gothick really came into its own during the course of the nineteenth century. The Chinese style, which was the gayest and most extreme fashion of the time, enjoyed its greatest popularity during the 1750s and disappeared almost as swiftly as it had appeared, returning only briefly during the nineteenth century Regency period. By the 1760s, the impetus of the Neoclassical revival was beginning to be felt, and with its advent the Rococo style in England abruptly disappeared.

Italy

The Rococo was never as enthusiastically developed in Italy as it was in France, and during the eighteenth century the outstanding features of the Baroque persisted. The Italian rich adored splendour and *grandezza*, and were by no means ready to relinquish their magnificent formality for the greater luxury, charm, and intimacy of the Rococo. State rooms continued to be of great importance in Italian palaces, and many of them were still decorated in the grand manner associated with the Baroque period. This, in part, explains the almost imperceptible transition from Baroque to Rococo in Italian furniture and architecture. Indeed, no such transition took place at all in some instances, so that in many grand rooms the Baroque reigned unperturbed until the advent of Neoclassicism. But, as in France, smaller, more intimate rooms did become less sparsely furnished than they had been. More comfortable furniture was found in the private apartments of the declining aristocracy, as well as in the increasingly prosperous homes of the rising professional and middle classes.

Italy was as politically fragmented in the eighteenth century as it had been in the seventeenth. Thus there were several centres of patronage, and the characteristics of furniture tended to vary from region to region. Rome was no longer the main source of influence, as it had been in the seventeenth century. Instead, the cultural guidelines laid down by France, especially Paris, exerted the strongest influence on the Rococo style in Italy, especially in the northern states, such as Piedmont. In 1734 the southern kingdom of Naples came under Bourbon rule and the new King, Charles III, was quick to establish porcelain and tapestry factories to furnish his various royal palaces in the style of the French royal patrons. In Lombardy, and particularly in its capital Milan, the influence of the imperial Austrian court predominated from the time of Austrian control in 1717. Furniture of the region became heavier, in contrast to the lighter, more restrained forms of Genoa.

At the same time, the Italian tradition of carving remained strong. The heavy sculptural forms of furniture in the Baroque style continued to

RIGHT *The bureau-bookcase was a form first popularized in England and Holland, but the curvilinear outline and vigorous design of this mid-eighteenth-century example in burr walnut suggest that it was made in Venice. Though modelled on late seventeenth- and early eighteenth-century types, its gilt-bronze mounts indicate a familiarity with contemporary Rococo decoration.*

find favour in Italian palaces. Although Antonio Corradini, inheritor of the great tradition established by the Venetian sculptor Brustolon, was working with a lighter touch by the turn of the century, his works were still monumental, essentially Baroque pieces intended for display. It was only very gradually that the profusely carved and gilded console

FAR LEFT *A profusely decorated cabinet, one of several similar pieces executed by Pietro Piffetti for the Royal House of Savoy in 1732. Piffetti was the finest cabinet-maker in Turin and may well have collaborated with the bronze sculptor Francesco Ladatte on the cabinet. The elaborate polychrome marquetry is set within an ebony framework, and includes a number of materials such as figwood, boxwood, mother-of-pearl and ivory.*

NEAR LEFT *Pietro Piffetti made this medal cabinet, decorated with a variety of rare, light-coloured woods and ivory, and portraying the seasons on the front two panels under the pair of glass doors. The very delicate form of the supporting table is typical of Piffetti's work.*

tables and the stately throne-like chairs became lighter in appearance, revealing greater freedom of movement in their overall design. Books of ornaments, such as that published by J. A. Meissonnier in 1734, may have helped to introduce Rococo forms to Italy, and gradually curves, scrolls and rockwork decoration began to be used on crestings and borders around panels, on commodes and cupboards. These were generally carved from wood and gilded, rather than cast in bronze and gilded, as in France. But there was one fine French-trained *ciseleur*, Francesco Ladatte, who worked for the court of Savoy, in Turin.

Turin, in the Piedmont, was one of the important centres in Italy during the Rococo period, from the turn of the century to about 1750. The Duke Vittorio Amadeo II assumed kingship in 1713. In 1714, he appointed Filippo Juvarra (1678–1736) Court Architect of the House of Savoy. Juvarra travelled extensively, and it is probable that in 1719 he passed through Paris, saw the Rococo style as it began to emerge there, and transmitted it to Italy. He worked for the court for twenty-two years, and his output was enormous. Apart from a number of town-planning schemes, including four town palaces and several churches, he was responsible for designing four royal residences, including the hunting lodge at Stupinigi which is one of the finest Rococo buildings in Italy. Although outside the architecture is of almost classical simplicity, the interior decoration is a breathtaking vision of spatial articulation and brilliant colour. Working very much in the manner of architect-designers elsewhere in Europe, Juvarra was responsible for bringing together some of the finest craftsmen ever assembled under one roof. There was Francesco Ladatte (1706–87), who was appointed Court Architect in 1745; there was Carlo Guiseppe Plura, (1655–1737), whose sculptures in wood were among the finest of the Turin school; and there was the *ébéniste* Pietro Piffetti (c. 1700–1777) who had previously worked in Rome. Piffetti was one of the few truly fine *ébénistes* in Italy, and the richness of his marquetried furniture was matched only by the lavishness of Juvarra's gilded and highly decorated interiors. A wide and varied range of materials was required for Piffetti's elaborate floral decorations. He executed a number of pieces designed by Juvarra. Juvarra had previously worked as a stage-set designer, and his interiors were well suited to house Piffetti's fantastic furnishings. Piffetti also made some fairly simple pieces, including a very attractive card-table decorated with a *trompe l'oeil* top of playing cards. Other typical pieces of eighteenth-century Italian furniture which were made in the palace workshops were ornate console tables, chairs, and carved and gilded mirrors.

The range of furniture used in Italy was never quite so exhaustive as that used in France. But there were some new pieces, like the prie-dieu (which, though created for use in a private chapel, also came to be used as

bedroom furniture), and the delicate *trespolo*, or tripod table, designed to support a mirror.

Though France's influence on Italian furniture design was important, ideas also came from England, Holland and Germany, which at that time still controlled the northern states of Venetia and Lombardy. Large, imposing bureaux surmounted by cabinets, modelled on Dutch and English bureaux, were extensively made in Italy. The heavier *bombé* form used on German and Dutch bureaux was also found in Italian pieces, especially in Naples and the south, which had previously been under Hapsburg domination. Such pieces were frequently lacquered and chinoiserie decoration, similar to that used in England and Holland, was popular. Sofas also became popular in Italy during the eighteenth century, and many of them are fine examples of Rococo flamboyance and frivolity. A set designed for the throne room of the Madama Reale, in Turin, shows a fine mastery of Rococo asymmetric and scrolling forms, while other sofas reflect the elegant sinuous lines of French Rococo furniture, and are carved with rockwork and acanthus leaf decoration.

The commode was also considered an important piece of furniture in eighteenth-century Italy. The French *bombé* form was adopted, notably in Venice, and exaggerated to become almost voluptuous, bulging outward at the top and slimming right down at the skirt to end in rather short, spindly but elegant cabriole legs. Such pieces were frequently decorated with colourful sprigs and festoons of flowers, landscapes and even religious scenes, and the borders were elegantly carved and gilded. Commodes from Genoa were decorated with simpler parquetry patterns

ABOVE *One of a set of ten settees designed to line the walls of the Throne Room in the Madama Reale, the palace in Turin of the King of Savoy. The early assimilation of French Rococo forms in the main centres of the northern Italian states can be seen in the vigorously confident way that the 'C' scrolls and rocaille work are handled in this piece. Large settees like this were also made for ballrooms.*

which were typical of the restrained elegance of much of the furniture coming from that republic.

Colour had always played an important part in Italian furniture decoration. *Pietre dure* remained the speciality of Florence, though much of Florence's workshops' output was destined for export, particularly to England, where it was highly prized. Scagliola, which was a less expensive imitation of *pietre dure*, continued to be much used on table tops and for pictures, and these too were sold abroad. Painted or japanned (*lacca*) furniture was extremely fashionable. In Southern Italy, a technique using a very thin coat of lacquer was developed. This allowed the grain of the wood to show through, and gave the piece an attractive, rustic look. Another inexpensive technique, mainly practised in Venice, was *lacca contrafetta*. This method involved painting the piece of furniture, and then pasting paper cut-outs on to its panels. The cut-outs were brightly painted pictures or coloured engravings, often of pastoral scenes, and after they were glued down, the whole piece of furniture was given a top coat of varnish.

From the richly massive carving of Turin to the light and bright *lacca*

BELOW *An elaborately shaped and carved commode, a fine example of the high bombé forms fashionable in Italy, particularly Venice, in the eighteenth century. Lacquer, or lacca, decoration was also a popular medium in Venice, and was widely used on all types of furniture. The painted floral sprays are set within carved and gilded Rococo panels. Although such pieces were influenced by French examples, the top-heavy appearance of this one makes it distinctly Italian.*

contrafetta of Venice, Italian Rococo exhibited almost as many different styles as there were states. Characterized by its very diversity, having no definite beginning nor conclusive ending, the Rococo period in Italy could perhaps be seen simply as Baroque at play, or Baroque relaxed.

Germany and Austria

In the eighteenth century, the northern states of Germany were mainly Protestant, the wealthy were middle-class merchants rather than aristocrats, and the furniture was basically traditional, though somewhat influenced by Dutch and English fashions.

The southern states were Catholic, and were divided, as they had been in the seventeenth century, between secular and ecclesiastical principalities and kingdoms. There were intense political and cultural rivalries among the various courts in the south. France exerted a very strong influence upon the development of the Rococo style in the south, and most of the furniture made for the more prominent German and Austrian courts of the eighteenth century was in imitation of models being produced in Paris. Thus at the Hapsburg court at Vienna, until the reign of Empress Maria Theresa, French fashions were copied and French cabinet-makers were employed.

French Rococo fashions were disseminated in the south through pattern books by designers such as Franz Habermann, then being published in the

ABOVE *The Spiegelsaal (Hall of Mirrors) is one of the finest examples of Rococo decoration in Germany. Designed by the Bavarian court architect, François Cuvilliés, the stucco decoration is the work of Johann Baptist Zimmerman. The room is one of the most handsome in the Amalienburg, a small garden palace built between 1734 and 1739, set in the grounds of Schloss Nymphenburg, residence of the Electors of Bavaria.*

great printing centre of Augsburg. French ideas were also brought to Germany by many designers and architects who, after about 1720, travelled to Paris to study the most recent developments there. The innovations of French ornamentalists and designers such as Meissonnier and Pineau and of furniture-makers like Charles Cressent were quickly adapted to suit German tastes. It was the aspect of fantasy in Rococo which fascinated the princes of Germany, and Rococo forms were employed to enhance the splendour of princely palaces, rather than to lend intimacy to interiors.

Among the most outstanding German Rococo designers was Flemish-born François Cuvilliés (1695–1768). Cuvilliés was first patronised by the Elector, Max Emanuel of Bavaria. Bavaria, with its court centred at Munich, had long been established as one of the most powerful German courts. Cuvilliés had first been employed as the court dwarf, but his talent was soon discovered, and he was sent to Paris to study under Blondel from 1720 to 1724. After his return to the Bavarian court, where the court architect, Effner, had already introduced the Rococo style, Cuvilliés published designs for interior schemes and for furniture which had enormous influence, particularly in Southern Germany but also in France and England. Among his finest creations were the designs for the interior of the Amalienburg Pavilion, a small hunting lodge set in the grounds of the Nymphenburg Palace. The mirrors in the *spiegelsaal* (hall of mirrors), sparkled against a background of blue and silver rocaille decoration, creating an effect of rare brilliance. The delicately trailing tendrils on the wall panels, or *boiseries*, are similar to the exquisitely carved forms used to decorate the famous commode thought to be

BELOW   *This famous commode was carved in 1761 by the Bavarian Johann Adam Pichler to a design by the dwarf architect-designer François Cuvilliés, The elegance and superb design of the commode illustrate Cuvilliés' understanding of French Rococo design, although the use of carved and gilded decoration of wood rather than ormolu mounts is a peculiarly German feature.*

designed by Cuvilliés and executed by the carver Johann Adam Pichler in 1761. This commode typifies the Bavarian preference for carved and gilded wood, which in its effect was similar to, but lighter than, French ormolu decoration. White painted backgrounds were often used in both interiors and on furniture to give prominence to the gilt Rococo decoration. But generally, the German princes tended to favour somewhat gaudier colours than their French counterparts, though, in the later years of the Rococo period, increasingly subtle nuances of colour and design were achieved.

The magnificent residence of the Prince Bishops at Würzburg was begun early in the eighteenth century. It was conceived in the splendid tradition of the late Baroque style, but the time taken to complete both the building and the interior decoration makes it a fascinating record of the changing styles in German decoration. The brilliance of its interiors was reflected in its furniture, which included some of the most flamboyant examples of Baroque and Rococo work to be found in Germany, like the carved pieces of the sculptor Franz Anton von Schlott, and the richly ornate cabinets of Carl Maximilian Mattern. Mattern's cabinets are extremely heavy in appearance, though ivory and mother-of-pearl in the

ABOVE LEFT *This exuberantly decorated silver andiron is characteristic of the German Rococo style, in which rocaille work or* muschelwerk *was often more exaggerated than elsewhere. This example was made by Philip Jacob Drenwelt of Augsburg between 1747 and 1749.*

ABOVE *A mid-eighteenth-century South German walnut* bombé bureau *inlaid with pewter, brass and tortoiseshell. The cartouche-shaped panel on the sloping flap is framed by foliate scrolls and strapwork borders. The engravings depict stories from the Bible, hunting scenes and landscapes.*

LEFT *The parade of rooms, just visible through the open door, is the setting chosen by the painter J. V. Tischbein in which to portray Count Vries and his family. The room is sparsely furnished by today's standards, but its elegance is evident in the finely carved Rococo boiseries showing French influence, and the inlaid floor. The room behind is even more luxurious and is hung with what is probably a blue damask which is also used to upholster the suite of chairs, just visible. The panel painting above the door is set in an elaborately carved frame. English influences appear in the hoop-backed design of the chairs, the table and the stool.*

marquetry decoration do somewhat lighten these otherwise essentially Baroque forms. In the neighbouring court of Bamberg, heavy *bombé* shapes were much in vogue on case furniture.

The furniture of the generally Protestant communities of the north tended to be functional rather than decorative, and was much more traditional. But Dutch and English influences were evident in a variety of chairs, which had hoop- or splat-back conformations and which were generally caned. The two-tiered cupboard was introduced in the eighteenth century, but it remained utilitarian rather than decorative until well into the century. This form of a chest of drawers surmounted by a two-door cupboard shows Anglo-Dutch influence but its heavy, often *bombé* shape reveals its Germanic derivation. By the middle of the century, attempts to lighten such pieces to conform more closely to the Rococo style led to the superficial application of Rococo decoration. Marquetry, or intarsia, using mother-of-pearl and precious metals, enjoyed a revival throughout Germany at this time. It gave a particularly rich effect when used on large cabinets.

Although many of the important centres were dominated by tradition-bound guild systems, an entrepreneurial cabinet-maker called Abraham

RIGHT *A large walnut bureau-cabinet derived from a type similar in both Holland and England since the early eighteenth century.*

RIGHT *Abraham Roentgen made this piece, which is in cherrywood and is finely carved around the apron and the legs, in about 1755.*

BELOW *A boldly carved walnut armchair made for the court of Frederick the Great of Prussia in about 1765. It is similar to the armchairs popular in Paris in the mid-eighteenth century.*

Roentgen established a workshop at Nieuwied, which was not restricted by regulations. Roentgen opened his workshop on the Rhine in 1750, on returning from a tour of England and Holland. Describing himself as an English cabinet-maker, he introduced many English furniture forms, and had considerable influence on German furniture in the middle of the eighteenth century.

The Saxon Court of the Elector, Augustus the Strong, had its principle residences in and around the confines of the city of Dresden and included both the older Palace of Moritzburg and the newer Zwinger Palace begun by Augustus in 1711. Dresden was the cultural and political centre of Saxony and it was just outside the city, at Meissen, that the famous porcelain factory was begun under Augustus' personal patronage in 1734. Much of the work produced in the factory was destined for his Japanese Palace in Dresden, in which he also displayed his extensive collection of Chinese and Japanese porcelain. Interest in oriental and chinoiserie decoration was prevalent throughout the Rococo period. The influence of English cabinet work was also evident in Saxon furniture-making, in the two-tier cabinets and cane-back chairs made for the Palace of Moritzburg. Until the Seven Years War (1756–63), Saxony's importance in Germany was considerable. But after being overrun and defeated by her northerly neighbour, Prussia, she never recovered her prestige and prosperity.

Under the powerful military leadership of Frederick the Great (1712–86), Prussia emerged in the second half of the eighteenth century as the dominant force in northern Germany. On his death, Frederick left behind a powerful and wealthy nation which had, during his lifetime, doubled in both size and population. But Frederick was also an important patron of the arts, so Prussia in his day became, as Voltaire described it, 'both a Sparta and an Athens'. His accession in 1740 marked the beginning of the development of the Rococo style in Prussia. Although the official residence of the monarch was Schloss Charlottenburg, Berlin, to which he added a magnificent west wing, his favourite scheme was the building of his summer palace at Schloss Sanssouci not far from Potsdam, the plans for which were drawn up in 1744. In participation with his court architect, George Wenzeslaus von Knobelsdorff (1699–1753), the king took great personal interest in such schemes. Created Superintendent of Palaces and Gardens in 1740, von Knobelsdorff was responsible for bringing together an important team of artists and designers whose works, although heavier and more vigorous than those of Cuvilliés in Munich, are among the finest examples of German Rococo furniture and decoration. Some of the finest furniture was carved by the wood-carver and sculptor Johann August Nahl, but he argued with Frederick in 1746, four years after his arrival, and fled. That year von Knobelsdorff also

quarrelled with the king and retired into obscurity until his death seven years later. Of the other artists and craftsmen who worked for the Prussian court, the best known were Johann Melchior Kambli, who had replaced Nahl, and the Hoppenhaupt brothers. Later in 1746, they were joined by the Spindler brothers who had worked for the smaller court at Bayreuth, further south.

The Low Countries

During the eighteenth century, there was a continual and rapid rise in the prosperity of the middle class in the Low Countries, particularly notice-able in Holland. Amsterdam, the centre of Dutch trade and commerce,

ABOVE *An extraordinary writing-desk from the Roentgen workshop, Neuwied, in the Rhineland, established by Abraham Roentgen in 1750. In the 1730s he had worked in London and subsequently described himself as an 'English cabinet-maker'. The elaborate pictorial marquetry work is superbly set off in the lively Rococo composition.*

continued to flourish. After the death of the Stadtholder William (also William III of England) in 1702, the Dutch burghers chose not to elect another stadtholder until the middle of the century. It was therefore the middle-class burghers, some having made great fortunes in distant colonies such as Java, who were responsible for stimulating new trends

and fashions in Holland during the eighteenth century. But generally, Dutch furniture declined in quality and originality after the seventeenth century.

The Rococo style did not affect Dutch furniture designs until well into the middle of the century. Though a great deal of Rococo furniture was imported from France and England, Dutch furniture of the Rococo period is markedly conservative and shows a preference for traditional forms. On seat furniture this is particularly noticeable. Many chairs retain, for instance, the claw and ball feet, which were outmoded in England. Marquetry decoration, which had so distinguished Dutch furniture in the previous century, was also maintained, and was used to decorate back splats on chairs as well as newly fashionable corner cabinets and French-inspired commodes. By the mid-eighteenth century,

however, the high standards of earlier *marqueteurs* had declined and the new marquetry work lacked the vitality of the marquetry seen on earlier, Baroque pieces. One of the better-known cabinet-makers working in the Rococo style, who made commodes in the French manner, was A. Bongen, who had a workshop in Amsterdam.

Throughout the eighteenth century, one of the most popular and stylish pieces made was the very large structure consisting of a chest of drawers surmounted by a two-door cabinet which fitted on top. The form of the bureau-bookcase was also sometimes appropriated to conceal a more utilitarian item, such as the household linen press. This type of deception itself indicates the social importance attached to such pieces, which were generally displayed in a prominent position.

In Holland the interiors of cabinets and cupboards were often painted, but it is not known whether this was done by furniture-makers or by the housewives. Generally, these pieces are wider and heavier in appearance than the English pieces from which they derive, and the introduction of *bombé* and serpentine shapes makes them more similar to northern German pieces. Rococo decoration might be introduced in the form of a curvilinear outline or a lively carved design on the panelling.

Some of the liveliest carving came from the workshops of Liège where the carver and furniture-maker Louis Lejeune produced some fine pieces. Liège, now a part of modern Belgium, was, in the eighteenth century, part of the Holy Roman Empire, and its close proximity to France led to French Rococo influences being quickly absorbed. The craftsmen there were famous for their bureau-bookcases, and for cupboards, longcase clocks and commodes. Like the Dutch, these craftsmen rarely used ormolu mounts to decorate their pieces but relied on carved decoration. Their work, however, is distinguished by a lightness and brilliance not seen in Dutch pieces, but which bears a close resemblance to work found on French *boiseries* (wall panels). This carving was done in a very hard, close-grained type of oak and required exceptional skill on the part of the carvers.

Holland had grown rich through her trading with the orient, and the influence of Chinese decoration was evident in Holland as it was elsewhere in Europe during the Rococo period. Door panels of cabinets, chests, and bureau-bookcases were decorated with real or imitation chinoiseries. Exquisitely painted mirror panels, carefully shipped from China, were also occasionally used, as they were in England, although their prohibitive cost made these rare items. Porcelain continued to be collected and was given pride of place in many rooms. Cornices on cupboards and cabinets continued to be elaborately stepped so as to provide small platforms for such pieces.

The popularity which tea-drinking had assumed in the eighteenth century led to a number of smaller pieces being made, especially tea-tables. These are generally heavier and more *bombé* in outline than English tea-tables, but the delicate, protective rails found on them, or on their accompanying trays, were often carved and pierced with delicacy and imagination.

North America

Rococo was the style dominant in America from about 1760 until the Revolution in 1776. Rococo in fact came to the colonies from England, where it was already on the decline, but the style was French in origin, as well as in spirit, and so in America it was optimistically labelled 'the new French style' (though retrospectively it was to be somewhat more

RIGHT *A highboy, made by John Pimm for the Loring family of Boston, in about 1750, which reflects English fashions of some thirty years earlier and demonstrates the slow transmission of ideas from Europe to America in the first half of the eighteenth century. It is made of local timber, and japanned in the Oriental fashion to simulate tortoiseshell. The hooded pediment and the cabriole legs are elegant features of American Queen Anne furniture.*

RIGHT *The
widespread use of English
pattern books in America
led to a remarkable affinity
between American and
English furniture during the
late eighteenth century. This
is borne out by the furniture
and the decoration of this
fashionable country house,
built in 1762 for the
prosperous Philadelphia
merchant, Edward Stiles.*

accurately described as 'American Chippendale'). The main centres of furniture production along the eastern seaboard were, respectively, Philadelphia in the middle, Newport and Boston in the north, and Charleston in the south, and each of these regions, during the course of time, developed its own highly individual style.

The furniture-making industry in eighteenth-century America thrived despite the vigorous opposition of the English government. Notwithstanding the restrictions imposed by the government on the expansion of local crafts and industries, the constant shortage of labour in the colonies and the promise of instant markets there spurred adventurous craftsmen from England and the Continent to emigrate to America, and there develop their skills. Parliamentary prohibitions did hinder the development of many specialized crafts, and it was necessary for the colonies to import such items as glass, brass (especially necessary for handles and escutcheons), bronze, and luxurious fabrics.

Throughout the eighteenth century, English furniture continued to be imported and imitated, but gradually actual importations came to be less heavily relied upon as sources of inspiration, with the growing number of local craftsmen. The occasional arrival of highly trained cabinet-makers such as Thomas Affleck who reached Philadelphia in 1763, helped not only to meet the demands of a rapidly growing population, but also to bring to America new ideas and fashions. Such men advertised themselves as being 'lately from London'. Apart from these new arrivals, the most important influence on American furniture was the publication of pattern books. These had been influential in America since the beginning of the century, but none was to be so widely examined and used as *The Gentleman and Cabinet-Maker's Director*, published in England first in 1754, again the following year, and finally, with new additions, in 1762.

Philadelphia was undoubtedly the most sophisticated city of eighteenth-century America, and the one which reflected most closely the fashions and tastes of Europe (though even Philadelphia was about twenty years behind her European counterparts). Rococo, which came into fashion around 1760, was the style used to decorate the houses and furniture of the wealthiest merchants and landowners of the city. Philadelphia was noted for its large and prosperous furniture-making industry. Among the most important furniture-makers working in the new Rococo style there were William Savery, Benjamin Randolph, Jonathan Shoemaker and Thomas Affleck.

In the north, some of the finest furniture was made by the interrelated Goddard and Townsend families, of Newport, Rhode Island. This large, extended family produced no less than twenty-one furniture-makers, and entirely dominated the craft in that region from the middle of the century until the Revolution. In general, furniture from the north was more conservative, more stylized and stiffer than that produced in Philadelphia during the same period.

The development of furniture-making in the south was perhaps hindered by the ease with which furniture could be imported from the north. It was shipped down the coast, in exchange for agricultural products such as corn and tobacco from the south. Thus, the prosperous homes of the southern colonists were, by and large, furnished with northern furniture. With the exception of Thomas Elfe, who had extensive premises in Charleston, and who is particularly noted for his fine fretwork, little is known of the established southern furniture-makers, though certainly there were some. One reason why so little is known is that the craft was frequently entrusted to slaves, who never became famous for it. Their training was often supervised by indentured servants, brought from England expressly for that purpose.

By the middle of the century, changing tastes, increasing wealth, and advancing technology created the demand for the importation of exotic timbers into America, such as mahogany, for mahogany was particularly well-suited to the fashions illustrated in Chippendale's *Director*. Mahogany was imported from Cuba, Santo Domingo and Honduras. But native woods, such as walnut, especially the black walnut grown in Virginia, cherry, and maple also remained popular. As in England, there was a preference for carved Rococo decoration, which allowed the natural grain of the wood to emerge as a decorative feature. Softer woods, such as birch and pine, were popular for more traditional country furniture, though walnut was generally used for the chests made by German immigrants who settled in Pennsylvania. These chests were usually decorated with stylized plant and animal forms, either painted in brilliant colours or inlaid, and were among the most colourful and decorative pieces of folk art to be made in America.

Compared with their European equivalents, prosperous American houses of the period were not large, but they were generally well-appointed, elegant, and above all comfortable, without being sumptuously luxurious. A wide range of articles was used to furnish them, many based closely on models from English pattern books, including Chippendale's *Director*, as well as books of the firms of Ince and Mayhew, Robert Mainwaring and Thomas Johnson, which were also well received in America. A piece copied from the pattern books typically tended to have a rather two-dimensional quality, as though the furniture were itself the embodiment of an engraving. This was a common flaw, and one which had characterized much European furniture during the sixteenth century.

Such a tendency was not present in the work of the most talented furniture-makers, like Benjamin Randolph of Philadelphia, whose elaborate trade card is distinctly similar to those exhibited and used by somewhat earlier London furniture-makers. The asymmetrical outline of the border, with its scrolls, and pierced and flaring forms, punctuated by birds and a most lifelike bust of a man, shows his very real under-standing of Rococo decorative motifs. In his furniture, such details are equally evident. His chairs and sofas do not exhibit the ponderous curves of the earlier, Baroque style. His top rails are exaggeratedly curved, incorporating the serpentine or 'cupid's bow' shape, which may have had its origin in China. This elaborately exaggerated use of the curved form was a dominant feature of Rococo. The cabriole leg, introduced around the middle of the century, remained popular on all forms of furniture, and was now generally finished off by the new addition of the claw and ball foot. Shell motifs entwined with acanthus leaf decoration and curly scrolling forms enlivened all kinds of surfaces. On chairs, back splats were pierced and carved.

Though furniture made in Philadelphia was generally more profusely carved and decorated than furniture made further north, the work of Thomas Affleck was somewhat austere. His style was typified by the straight 'Marlboro' leg, used on beds, chairs, tables, sofas and cabinets. The leg was often decorated with the type of blind fret carving associated with the Gothick and Chinese styles shown in Chippendale's *Director*.

Highboys, or high chests, were very fashionable in American households. During the first half of the century, New England had been dominant in the production of highboys, but around 1760, the lead was taken by Philadelphia. In conformation, Rococo highboys were similar to earlier models, but in the later part of the century they were often made from mahogany, which was the wood that lent itself best to decorative carving. Newly fashionable claw and ball feet were added, and legs were slightly shortened, and were frequently decorated with carved scallop shells to the knees. Highboys are among the finest examples of the craftsmanship of the period, and no elegant Philadelphia reception room was without one.

Secretary desks were also designed as showpieces. Some, like those made in the workshops of John Cogswell, in Boston, exhibited the *bombé*, or swollen profile on their lower sections, a form imported from Northern Germany or Holland. A distinctive feature of much of the case furniture made in Newport was blocking. This technique had its origins in seventeenth-century Europe, and was probably introduced into America by Dutch and German immigrants during the course of the eighteenth century. It was first recorded as being used by John Coit Jr. of Boston, on a fine secretary-desk–bookcase, but the method then became associated chiefly with the Townsend family in Newport. Blocking was the use of rounded, vertical, 'blocked' panels of wood, which were applied to the drawer fronts of most forms of case furniture. The result was a marked decorative contrast of undulating planes. The central panel was generally recessed, or concave, while those flanking it were convex in form. The shell motif, which by itself had been a feature on earlier Queen Anne models, was often used to decorate the top sections of all three panels, and even inside the recess. Blocking tended to create a rather stiff and formal effect.

Gilding was rarely used to decorate American Rococo furniture, though there is one white painted and gilded mirror made by James Reynolds for General Cadwalader which is among the finest American interpretations of Rococo, incorporating delicate sprays of flowers and foliage entwined with the lightest of scrolling forms.

Throughout the period, much of the furniture being made was still based on more traditional styles from the Queen Anne period. Windsor, or ladder-back chairs, for instance, were still very much used. It was mainly in the houses of successful merchants that the most up-to-date and fashionable examples of Rococo style were to be found. With the beginning of the Revolution, furniture production declined altogether. When the war ended, Neoclassicism took over, and Rococo virtually disappeared, its popularity having been as short-lived in America as it had been in England.

LEFT The *bureau plat* (writing table) was introduced at the beginning of the Rococo period in France. This example was made during the 1720s by Charles Cressent who was noted not only as an *ébéniste*, but also for the quality of his bronze mounts. Cressent's light handling of materials can be seen in this piece, which is veneered in the rich tones of tulipwood and kingwood.

BELOW A *fauteuil* (armchair) *à la reine* with its elegant straight back which is a complimentary reference to Louis XV's Queen, Marie Lesczynska. This carved and painted example is probably by Jean-Baptiste Cresson, a member of the large Cresson family which produced at least ten *maître menuisiers*, many of whom signed their work in the same way, leading to subsequent difficulties in attribution.

ABOVE An *encoignure*, or corner-cupboard, which was one of a pair made by Jacques Dubois. The segmental shape, necessary to fit the corner position, is generally tempered by the use of a bow-fronted door, as in this example. Veneered on oak (as all the best work was in France) in contrasting woods, the unusually symmetrical design of the bronze mounts centres on a mask of Diana. The top, like those of most French commodes during the eighteenth century, is of *breccia* marble.

LEFT Small tables became very popular in the mid-eighteenth century. One variety was the delicate *bonheur du jour*, which could be used as a small writing table, as a dressing table or even as a work table. The delicate framework often required the addition of a stretcher, and the top was surmounted by a small cabinet with pigeon holes and drawers. The form was much imitated abroad, and many were made in England in the last few decades of the eighteenth century. This one was made by one of the lesser known *petis maîtres*, Charles Topino.

BELOW A large bookcase cabinet with four dividing panels veneered in tortoiseshell and brass in the manner of Boulle. Boulle work, despite its heavy, ornate appearance, continued to be fashionable throughout the eighteenth century, and original pieces by the old master fetched consistently high prices at auctions. Boulle died in 1732, but his workshop was continued by his sons. This piece was made by Etienne Levasseur, a pupil of the younger Boulle. Levasseur became a *maître ébéniste* in 1767. Although dating from the Rococo period, this piece demonstrates the conservative taste of some patrons which was always present.

BELOW A pendulum clock, with a complex astronomical movement, contained in a superb gilt bronze frame and supported on a decorated base veneered in purplewood. The marquetried central panel is worked on a ground of sycamore wood, although this may be a later addition. The clock is attributed to Alexandre Fortier. Bronze figures in the form of putti and 'Time' surmount the top of the clock.

LEFT   A side table and mirror designed by Mathias Lock, who also did much of the carving. Made in about 1745, they show, despite their somewhat heavy form, Lock's complete understanding of the Rococo style, and are among the most important examples of the early English Rococo. Originally made *en suite* with a pair of flanking candlestands, notes on the side of the original sketches show that the table took 89 days to make and the mirror frame 138, of which Lock himself contributed twenty.

BELOW   A side table and matching mirror, made around 1755, in the Gothick style. The severe rectilinear outline of this quasi-architectural style is relieved by the addition of 'C' scrolls, and in their delicacy and lightness, the pieces are thoroughly Rococo. The striking colour contrast is achieved by the use of ebonized and gilded pine. The Gothick revival style was peculiar to Britain at this date.

ABOVE LEFT   A small corner cabinet decorated with floral marquetry on a dark chestnut ground. It was made by the German cabinet-maker F. Reizell who worked for the Prince de Condé and spent much of his time in Paris.

LEFT   A small commode, one of a pair made by Nicholas Jean Marchand for Louis XV's Queen, at the Chateau de Fontainebleau. The framework is of ebony, and the panels on the sides are probably Japanese lacquer work, while the front panel is a European imitation of Oriental work. As on most French commodes, the top is of marble. The light curvilinear outline of the piece makes it a fine example of eighteenth-century Rococo furniture.

LEFT An elaborately carved mahogany stool demonstrating the importance attached to stools until well into the eighteenth century, when strict rules of etiquette entitled only the reigning monarchs and the heir presumptive to sit on chairs. This fine stool is vigorously carved with foliage and the legs end in fishy scales and dolphin feet.

LEFT The taste for the exotic was one aspect of English Rococo style. This, the Chinese Room at Claydon, is one of the most extraordinary interior decoration schemes in England. The elaborately carved and pierced pagoda-shaped alcove is made entirely of wood. This alcove now houses a sumptuously upholstered divan, but the furniture depicted in the photograph is mostly Oriental and of different periods. The bamboo sofa and the centre table shown are of Cantonese origin.

BELOW Standing shelves, like hanging shelves, do not seem to have been widely used before 1750, but for the rest of the century they were frequently illustrated in the work of designers. This set is japanned and decorated in the Oriental fashion; carved and painted shelves were also popular. They were intended to display china, books and small objets d'art, and were occasionally made in pairs. This one is similar to a design in Chippendale's *Director*.

FAR LEFT A finely carved mahogany chair in Chippendale's 'Chinese' style. In the *Director*, Chippendale comments that the chairs are 'very proper for a Lady's Dressing Room' or 'will likewise suit Chinese Temples'. This chair has a drop-in seat upholstered in black horse-hair fabric, which was then fashionable and extremely hard-wearing.

LEFT A carved mahogany candlestand which is similar to several designs in Chippendale's *Director*. This example reflects the lighter forms of the Rococo style, and makes full use of delicately curved 'C' and 'S' forms. Candlestands were designed to support the candelabra, which were the main form of illumination in the eighteenth century.

LEFT   A room of painted silk at the hunting lodge at Stupinigi, near Turin. The lightness and freshness of this interior indicate that the architect Filippo Juvarra was fully cognizant of the international Rococo style.

LEFT The use of Chinese lacquer panels to decorate Rococo interiors was extremely expensive, since each panel had to be either specially imported, or removed from imported lacquer furniture. The Chinese room at the Palazzo Reale in Turin was designed by the court architect Filippo Juvarra in 1735.

ABOVE This elegantly carved and gilded sofa demonstrates the high standards achieved by Italian wood carvers. The luxury of the piece is emphasized by its silk upholstery. Seat furniture of this type was generally made *en suite* with similar pieces.

BELOW A richly veneered chest of drawers in rosewood and tulipwood. The serpentine shape of the front contrasts with the angularity of the veneering which is set in a complex pattern of diagonals alternating occasionally with verticals, according to the placement of the wood's grain. The opposition of the diagonal veneers on the drawer fronts creates a pattern known as herringbone, or feather pattern. The top of this chest of drawers is decorated more elaborately with a medallion veneered in rare wood and tortoiseshell, and depicts the Rape of the Sabine Women.

LEFT A marquetry commode attributed to one of the finest Italian cabinet-makers of the eighteenth century, Giuseppe Maggiolini, whose workshop was in Milan. Despite the flamboyance of the *bombé* form, the commode is restrained in decoration. The ormolu handles, believed to have been made by the ornamentalist Giuseppe Levati, surround a central panel depicting an Oriental scene and Oriental scenes also feature on the two escutcheon plates.

LEFT   A sinuously carved candelabra, executed in both metal and wood. The carved and gilded figure of a dolphin is supported on a carved and painted rockwork base and illustrates the Italian preference for such furniture. The seven-branched candelabra delicately suspended on outcurved acanthus leaves is of gilded metal.

BELOW   This richly carved and gilded console table and mirror are good examples of the type of ostentatious furniture used to decorate the lavish state apartments of an eighteenth-century Genoese palace. The table is supported by four female figures, each representing one of the four seasons.

RIGHT This bureau-cabinet was made for the Danish King in 1755. Despite its Danish origin, it reflects the heavy opulence of contemporary German taste, the principal source of influence in Denmark at that time. The elaborate complexity of the piece with its remarkable curvilinear outline, kingwood parquetry and inlay in bone and ivory on metal combined with the ebulliently carved rocaille enrichments illustrate the extensive skills of its maker C. F. Lehmann.

The Neoclassical Period

T HE NEOCLASSICAL STYLE BEGAN to be evident in Europe by the middle of the eighteenth century. In France and England, Neoclassicism was already fashionable by the 1760s. But elsewhere it only gradually gained momentum and was not widely established as an international style, in both Europe and America, until the 1780s.

Neoclassicism came into vogue in France and England as a reaction to the excesses of the Rococo, but the style itself was the result of a growing international interest in contemporary archaeological discoveries. The style was symptomatic of a new philosophical outlook which regarded the Rococo as synonymous with the hedonism and superficiality of an aristocratic society dedicated to the pursuit of pleasure. There was, in Neoclassicism, a strong moralizing element. The Neoclassicists aimed to create a new society, one which would be pure, balanced and reasonable. This was to be partly achieved through the pure forms of Neoclassical art, which, in their serene simplicity, were seen to be of moral value. Neoclassicism was essentially modern in what Sir John Summerson has called its 'idealisation of the future' and in its self-conscious attempt to create a morally, spiritually and aesthetically superior society. 'There is only one way for the moderns to become great,' wrote one of Neoclassicism's greatest proponents, Johann Joachim Winckelmann, 'and that is by imitating the ancients.'

International interest in archaeology was greatly stimulated in the second quarter of the eighteenth century by excavations undertaken in Italy, Greece and in the far-flung colonies of ancient Rome such as Asia Minor. One of the most exciting excavations had been that of Herculaneum in 1738, later described by Goethe as the 'alpha and omega of all collections of antiques', and of Pompeii in 1748. By the middle of the century it was usual for those young men who undertook the grand tour to study at these various sites. For those unable to afford the tour, numerous publications appeared from the middle of the eighteenth century onwards, which provided superbly adequate visual impressions of the

RIGHT *During the second half of the eighteenth century in England, libraries had gradually developed into important reception rooms and were increasing in size. The library at Osterley Park, situated next to the formal state dining room, is on the ground floor of the house, thus emphasizing its importance. The carefully interrelated scheme of the room and the furniture is typical of Robert Adam's attention to detail. Adam even suggested the designs for the inset paintings on canvas, which were executed by the Italian, Antonio Zucchi.*

numerous and various domestic and civic treasures which were then being found.

Inevitably, in this climate of intellectual and philosophical ferment, disagreement arose concerning the superiority of Greek versus Roman classicism. Abbé Laugier, in France, a notable architectural theorist of early Neoclassicism, Winckelmann, in Germany, whose *Gedanken uber die Nachamung der Griechischen Werke*, published in 1755, was of seminal importance, and James 'Athenian' Stuart and Nicholas Revett in England were among the most vehement supporters of the earlier and simpler classical Greek forms. Abbé Laugier categorically stated in his *Essai sur l'architecture*, in 1753: 'Architecture owes all that is precious and solid to the Greeks alone.' In Rome, the other side of the argument was taken up by the bombastic Italian artist Giambattista Piranesi (1720–78), whose published drawings of the noble ruins of ancient Rome did much to inspire English Neoclassical developments.

The approach of the Neoclassicists became increasingly scientific and empirical, and by the beginning of the nineteenth century ornaments and forms were being copied directly from closely examined ancient examples. In France, Napoleon modelled his Empire on that of ancient

ABOVE *Thomas Chippendale made this side table in 1767 for the music room at Harewood House. It is one of the finest pieces ever to be produced in his workshop. In the Neoclassical style developed by James 'Athenian' Stuart and Robert Adam, it incorporates a number of motifs taken from the archaeological discoveries such as the formalized honeysuckle motif along the frieze and the graceful festoons of husks.*

Imperial Rome. This affected not only the political structure of the new France, but also all the decorative arts, including furniture-making. Egyptian artifacts too, though they were not classical, became popular as models, and were much imitated, after Baron Denon, who accompanied Napoleon on his Egyptian campaigns, published his *Voyage dans la Basse et Haute Egypte*, in 1802.

Neoclassicism continued to dominate the artistic direction of Europe and America throughout the first quarter of the nineteenth century, but by the 1830s the style had become somewhat stale and repetitive. With the advent of Romanticism, and a growing interest in the revival of various other historical styles, Neoclassicism gradually waned.

France

The style now known as 'Louis XVI' was already established by the time of Louis' accession in 1775, though it did not reach its maturity, or become accepted in court circles, until the first decade of his reign. Through the 1770s and 1780s, while the state of France generally was swiftly deteriorating, the court of Louis XVI and Marie Antoinette dazzled the European

world with its brilliance and lavishness. But the French Revolution began in 1789, bringing with it a reign of terror and bloodshed, and by the time the king and queen were executed, the style associated with their reign had suffered a demise as well, to be replaced by a much sterner form of Neoclassicism, the Empire style.

The last years of Louis XV witnessed the decline of the Rococo, and for a time there was a juxtaposition of Rococo with Neoclassicism, constituting what is now known as the transitional style. For although the waywardness of Rococo forms fascinated and amused the majority of the *haut monde* during the middle of the eighteenth century, there were a few who remained unmoved by Rococo's charm. They found Rococo ornamentation trivial to the point of decadence, and turned instead to the pure forms of classical antiquity for inspiration.

As early as 1749, Mme de Pompadour, the vivacious mistress of Louis XV, who was always keen to have a foretaste of anything new, as well as to promote her brother's fortunes, sent her brother (the future Marquis

ABOVE *A low breakfront cabinet, made up of three cupboards decorated with classical figures in relief. The signature 'Joseph' between two lilies appears under the slab on the right. This name was used by both Joseph Baumhauer and his son Gaspar Joseph Baumhauer. Stylistically the cabinet has been attributed to the son. The design of the feet, some of the frieze mounts and the use of large areas of plain brass marquetry mark this piece as more characteristic of the Neoclassical taste of the later eighteenth century.*

ABOVE *This low breakfronted book cabinet is divided into three sections, centring on an elaborately decorated panel veneered in tortoiseshell and brass. The central figure of Pomona is supported on a pedestal, surrounded by foliated marquetry and flanked by Neoclassical trophies. This cabinet is stamped twice with the name of the* maître ébéniste *Jean Louis Faizelot Delorme who was working from about 1763 to 1780.*

de Marigny) on a grand tour of Italy, to examine the antiquities which archaeologists had unearthed at Pompeii. He was accompanied by some of the most vigorous critics of the Rococo style, including the art critic, Abbé le Blanc, the architect, Soufflot, and the designer, Cochin. These men were ardently enthusiastic about their findings, and were to provide a vanguard movement for the new style of Neoclassicism in France. Another early advocate of Neoclassicism was the Comte de Caylus, whose book, *Recueil d'Antiquités*, which began to appear in 1752, gave a highly influential exposition of the subject. Caylus, along with other antiquarians, art lovers, and intellectuals (including Voltaire) deplored the frivolity of Rococo. They saw Neoclassicism not merely as a new fashion, but as a symbol of moral regeneration, based on the virtues of ancient Roman Republicanism, and exemplified in the stately lines of classical architecture and design.

Few examples of Neoclassicism were evident in furniture before 1760. But the decade between 1760 and 1770 was an important one for the

LEFT *An armchair, or fauteuil à la reine, of carved and painted wood, made for Queen Marie-Antoinette by one of the eighteenth century's famous cabinet- and chair-makers Georges Jacob, in 1787 at Versailles.*

BELOW *Marie-Antoinette's boudoir. This delicately decorated interior was painted by the Rousseau brothers in 1785. The style of the decoration is based on painting found at Pompeii. The superb bureau à cylindre was made by Jean Henri Reisener and is decorated with marquetry of mother-of-pearl, silver and bronze.*

development and formulation of the style. Confusingly, many pieces retained, at that time, their essentially Rococo curvilinear outlines, but they were adorned with Neoclassical ornamentation. A Rococo commode of *bombé* shape, with cabriole legs, might sport mounts with vitruvian or wavy-line scrolling, caryatids, lion heads, palm leaves, sphinxes, or a host of other ornaments reminiscent of classical antiquity.

Carving no longer showed the ebullience of Rococo carving, but was flatter, and more restrained. Gradually, the outlines of furniture, particularly case furniture, became more straight and angular. Marquetry returned to popularity, as it was well suited to this type of furniture, and pictorial and floral panels were exquisitely worked into the surface decoration of much case furniture, while vertical and horizontal lines were emphasized with superbly cast and gilded bronze mounts.

Despite Mme de Pompadour's enthusiasm, Neoclassicism did not become really fashionable in court circles until about 1770. A well-known water-colour sketch, done in 1771, celebrates the triumph of the new style in depicting a fête given by Mme de Pompadour's successor, Mme Du Barry, at her chateau at Louveciennes. Cabriole legs and serpentines are absent, having been replaced by thoroughly Neoclassical forms – straight, tapered legs, linear uprights, and superb bronze mounts.

BELOW   *Louis XVI's library at Versailles was designed by Jacques-Ange Gabriel. The work was carried out by Antoine Rousseau who also worked on a number of projects for Louis XVI's Queen, Marie-Antoinette. The royal fleur-de-lis motif was woven into the carpet. Chairs, à la reine, are deployed in a formal way, characteristic of the age, around the sides of the book-lined walls. The magnificent circular centre table was made by Roentgen and is of sequoia wood.*

One of the finest *marqueteurs* working for the court of Louis XV during the middle of the century was Jean François Oeben (c. 1715–63). Trained in the workshops of the legendary Boulle, Oeben continued the mag-

LEFT *One of the earliest pieces of furniture to be made in the Neoclassical style is this ornately decorated* bureau plat *designed by Louis Joseph Le Lorrain for Lalive de Jully's cabinet. The heavy patterns of the ormolu work, such as the Greek key pattern, and the use of Vitruvian scrolling are reminiscent of the formal, ornate designs fashionable in early eighteenth-century English Palladian circles. The bureau, with the cartonnier which stands at one end to hold writing materials, was made under the supervision of Caffieri in about 1756.*

nificent marquetry tradition which the old master had established. Oeben's greatest contribution was to develop the pictorial marquetry typical of the transitional period. When Oeben died, he was succeeded by his pupil, Jean Henri Riesener (1734–1806). Riesener married Oeben's widow, took over his workshops, and then went on to produce some of the finest marquetried pieces ever to be executed. Appointed to the court in 1775, Riesener was fortunate enough to be *Ebéniste du Roi* at a time when court expenditure on furniture was higher than ever before. This gave him the opportunity to develop his work, which was highly individual, although he worked in the tradition of the transitional style until about 1775, when his forms became heavier and his marquetry more restrained. The lozenge-shaped marquetry enclosing a repeated flower motif is typical of his work. Another *ébéniste* who had worked with Oeben was Jean François Leleu. Like Oeben, he designed *tables à transformation* (mechanical tables) which fascinated Louis XVI. Martin Carlin too was a fine *ébéniste* who worked for the court, and his brother-in-law was also an *ébéniste*, Roger Lacroix. Close family links between craftsmen

RIGHT *A bow-fronted* secrétaire à abattant, *probably made by Martin Carlin in about 1766, which is the date mark found on the Sèvres porcelain plaques, and is also the year in which Carlin became an ébéniste. Although very little is known of the life of Carlin, he did make a few pieces for Queen Marie-Antoinette and for the King's aunts. He appears to have worked chiefly for the powerful* marchands-merciers *and almost certainly for Simon-Philippe Poirier, who held a virtual monopoly of both Sèvres porcelain plaques and imported Oriental lacquer. Carlin's fondness for using both porcelain and lacquer in his work was probably encouraged by Poirier.*

LEFT *A magnificent cabinet fitted with drawers below and surmounted by a clock, which was made either by Martin Carlin or Jean-François Leleu, since it carries both these ébénistes' stamps. It was common practice for an ébéniste who was employed to repair or reconstruct an item of fine furniture to add his own stamp to the piece, thus giving rise to considerable confusion in attribution. At some time this piece was substantially altered by one or other of these ébénistes. By 1760, Sèvres plaques were being used in furniture and the thirty plaques incorporated in this piece were made in 1760. Their brilliant green and white colouring is set off by the equally vivid colouring of the tulipwood veneer.*

ABOVE RIGHT *This elegant little table is one example of the many varied types of small tables which were popularized during the second half of the eighteenth century. Neat, light and compact, it combines several functions and can be used as a writing-, reading- or work-table. The top, which incorporates a Sèvres porcelain plaque, can be raised at a slant to become a bookrest. Alternatively, the whole top can be raised on ratchets to reveal a shallow tray. It was made by Martin Carlin probably in 1783, only two years before his death.*

ABOVE RIGHT *A small cabinet made by* maître ébéniste *Etienne Avril for Marie-Antoinette. The blue porcelain plaques enlivened with classical dancing female figures were made in the royal porcelain manufactory, at Sèvres, and reflect the simpler lines of the Neoclassical taste.*

were fairly common at that time, when the structure of society was of clearly defined close-knit strata.

Lacquer, and its cheaper imitation, *vernis Martin*, had been so integral a part of fashionable furniture throughout the eighteenth century that it never completely disappeared, though it was not particularly well suited to the increasingly severe Neoclassical idiom. Surface decorations which were more appropriate, and which were to become closely associated with the new style, were porcelain plaques, usually manufactured at the Royal Porcelain Factory at Sèvres. Appropriate or not, it appears that the success of the plaques was partly due to the promotional techniques of *marchands-merciers*. Poirier, who had a near monopoly on imported lacquer, held large supplies of porcelain in his stocks as well, and he employed *ébénistes* such as Martin Carlin to incorporate the plaques in the furniture. Poirier's power was passed on to the equally well-known Daguerre, who was also a middle-man for Carlin. The brightly

LEFT *France faced several economic crises in the decade before the Revolution in 1789. Opulent furniture gave way to plainer, simpler pieces which anticipated the Directoire style. This elegant elegant bureau à cylindre in mahogany is by Jean-Henri Riesener who had been responsible for completing the famous bureau du roi of Louis XV upon which this piece is loosely modelled.*

coloured plaques were exquisite in combination with the vivid colours of the interior schemes and marquetry. The marquetry has mostly faded now, but when freshly executed, the pictorial and geometric marquetry compositions of *ébénistes* like Riesener, Leleu, and Oeben must have been brilliant.

The increasingly austere economic climate in France during the last decade before the Revolution was reflected in the severity of Neoclassicism during that period. Forms became more linear, the relatively simple *secrétaire à abbatant* (a type of upright, drop-front desk), already popular, became more so, and elaborate decoration was generally abandoned in favour of plain veneering. Small tables were modelled on tables found on archaeological sites. *Athéniennes* (tripod stands) modelled on ancient perfume burners with wrought iron legs took the place of the elaborate *guéridons* which had long been popular.

Mahogany was only one of about fifty types of wood used by Parisian *ébénistes*. As had been the case throughout the eighteenth century, the carcass of the item of furniture to be veneered was generally made of a cheaper and inferior wood such as pine. Since much of the internal construction was not designed to be visible, there was a tendency, towards the end of the century, for standards of construction of French furniture

ABOVE RIGHT *This armchair, or* fauteuil à la reine, *is almost certainly part of a larger suite. In form it bears some similarity to the work of the* menuisier *Georges Jacob.*

ABOVE LEFT *This finely carved and gilded chair, in the early Neoclassical style, is by Louis Delanois. Delanois was a fashionable chair-maker and designer from the time he was made a master* menuisier *in 1761 until 1789.*

to drop, in some cases quite dramatically as effort and expense were devoted to the appearance of the piece.

Chairs made by the *menuisiers*, on the other hand, were fairly visible throughout. The most famous *menuisier* of the reign was Georges Jacob (1739–1814), who was probably the most important craftsman working for the court, except for the *ébéniste*, Riesener. Jacob executed the chairs designed by the painter Robert Hubert for Marie-Antoinette's dairy at Rambouillet, and was among the first to use mahogany in chair-making. He also introduced the sabre leg, or leg *à l'étrusque* into France. His work was sought after by English noblemen, such as the Prince of Wales and the Duke of Bedford, for whom he designed much furniture (commissioned through Daguerre).

As Neoclassicism took over, chairs gradually lost their delicate curvilinear shapes and gay embellishments. Instead, they became elegantly

refined, their overall outlines softened only by the use of oval-shaped backs and exquisitely carved Neoclassical motifs. Upholstery remained much as it had been during the previous period, but generally, lighter materials were used. The intimate lifestyle which had been the hallmark of the previous reign continued, and there were few innovations or additions to the extensive range of furniture types already in use at the beginning of the Neoclassical period.

The disruption caused by the Revolution had two serious effects on furniture production in France. First, the guild system was abolished in 1791. From the time of Louis XIV, the guild system had ensured at all times the highest possible standards of craftsmanship. Gradually, during the course of the nineteenth century, these standards were eroded, particularly as commercialism in craft industries increased. Secondly, the death of the monarch and the dispersion of the court meant that the major source of patronage for furniture-makers suddenly vanished. There was, to be sure, for a brief, glittering spell, a revival of patronage during the Empire period, particularly by the members of the imperial family, but never again was patronage to be the pillar of support for artists and craftsmen that it had been during the *ancien régime*.

The term used to describe the period from about 1795 to the time of Napoleon's coronation as emperor in 1804 is the Directoire. Named after

ABOVE *A voyeuse designed for a spectator to sit astride or kneel at; arms were rested on the padded top rail. This was considered a comfortable way to watch card games in particular.*

ABOVE LEFT *This stool is one of two types used particularly in court circles from the seventeenth century. This type of folding stool, described as a* pliant, *has an X-shaped frame, making it collapsible and easily portable. The other type of stool, the* tabouret, *was of a fixed, upright form and was not so commonly used.*

the successive governments which restored at least a semblance of peace to the country, it was not a period of great development or innovation in the arts. The predominantly Greek-influenced Neoclassicism which had characterized the reign of Louis XVI continued, as it was to continue, in modified form, throughout the first quarter of the nineteenth century. There was a tendency in furniture-making towards ever greater simplicity and less decoration, partly because of the economic stringencies of the time, and partly because those in power were not used to being the upholders of grand styles and fashion, as the members of the old aristocracy had been. Examples of the continuing Greek style at this time were the graceful roll-back chairs, and the elegant sabre legs which Jacob had introduced on furniture in the 1790s, and which presaged the Empire style.

Jacob was one of several furniture-makers of the old school to have survived the terrors of the Revolution. He re-emerged after the war was over, to hand on his valuable knowledge to a new generation of furniture-makers. This, for a time at least, ensured that some of the standards of craftsmanship upheld by the old regime were still preserved. Jacob retired in 1796, but his workshop continued under the direction of his sons, one of whom, under the assumed name Jacob Desmalter, was to become the most famous furniture-maker of the Empire period.

The interest in archaeology became increasingly widespread by the end of the eighteenth century. In 1795, Napoleon led a martial expedition to Egypt which lasted four years. One of the members of the expedition was Baron Dominique Vivant Denon, who went along to do archaeological research, and to record his findings. The result was his book,

G✦IACOB JACOB·FRERES RUE MESLEE **JACOB·D· R·MESLEE**

ABOVE *This* guéridon *is supported on three sabre-shaped legs, a martial device popular during this period.*

ABOVE RIGHT *A* secrétaire à abattant *made by Simon Mansion in 1813. The wide areas of finely matched mahogany veneers are relieved by fine ebony stringing lines, gilded bronze mounts in the form of classical trophies, and festoons of flowers along the frieze.*

Voyage dans la Basse et Haute Egypte pendant les campagnes du Générale Bonaparte. This book was largely responsible for the sudden upsurge of interest in things Egyptian. The *retour d'Egypte* was seen on furniture everywhere. Mummified figures, gods from the Egyptian pantheon, sphinxes and ancient pharaohs, mostly copied from the illustrations in Denon's book, became the most sought-after decorations of the day. Denon himself continued to have great influence in the arts, and was made Director of the Musée Napoléon and Master of the Mint.

Napoleon crowned himself emperor in 1804, and that year saw the emergence of the Empire style. The Empire style was Neoclassicism at its most academic and severe. Napoleon, who saw himself both as the Caesar of France, and as a second sun king, sought to create in his surroundings a second Imperial Rome, embellished by the formal trappings of

splendour associated with the court of Louis XIV. The informality which had prevailed during the reigns of Louis XV and Louis XVI disappeared. Comfortable furniture was replaced by furniture which conformed to the new, stringent, academic taste. Art, pressed into the service of the emperor, played an important part in the propagandist machinery of the period. The two most influential figures of the Empire style were the architect-designers Percier and Fontaine. All their work showed a unity of design and purpose. They had both spent time in Rome, studying original artifacts, and had concluded that it would 'be vain to seek for shapes preferable to those handed down to us by the ancients'.

With the increasingly purist approach to archaeology, pieces were modelled much more closely on the originals. Furniture became more massive, taking on a heroic monumentality. Light relief in the form of mouldings disappeared. Mounts were used starkly, and the angularity of a piece of furniture was frequently emphasized by the use of lozenge

ABOVE *Ancient Roman and Greek interiors were much imitated during the early nineteenth century. The stucco panels in this dining room at Malmaison, painted by Lafitte, are decorated with motifs based on ancient Pompeian models unearthed in excavations.*

or geometric shapes inlaid into the surface. Chair backs were stiff and square, and the legs of many chairs were shaped in the style found on Louis XIV chairs. Napoleon's military victories were announced on furniture in the forms of crossed swords, laurel crowns, bows, and arrows. Stools took the forms of drums, and interiors themselves were sometimes tented, as if on battlefields.

While most of the furniture of the period was heavy, grand and masculine, the emperor's beautiful wife, Joséphine, did introduce a few feminine motifs expressive of her own taste. Her favourite motif was the swan, and at Malmaison, the house she shared with Napoleon and in which she continued to live even after her divorce, many of the state rooms are decorated with swans. Swans were even incorporated into the structure of furniture, so that chair arms were in the form of swans, and beds and tables were supported by them.

There were a few magazines, such as Percier and Fontaine's *Recueil*

RIGHT *This elaborately shaped bed* en bateau *(in the shape of a boat) was designed as part of a larger suite of furniture for Pius VII at Fontainebleau. The boat form was highly fashionable for Empire beds, and the scroll ends were frequently featured on seat furniture. The bed may have been made by the Bellangés who, with the Lemarchands, the Mansions and Jacob Desmalter were amongst the foremost furniture-makers during the early nineteenth century.*

BELOW *The ormolu mounts on this mahogany lit* en bateau *depict two classical female figures and stars, and are surmounted by crisply carved winged sphinxes.*

des decorations intérieures, or Mesangère's *Collections des objets de goût*, which were important, as they are today, for disseminating the latest ideas and fashions to a larger public than before. But there were few new forms of furniture introduced during the Empire period. Two which had not been seen earlier were the delicate *table à toilette*, designed to be perched on a lady's knee, and the large Psyche mirror. Generally, however, there was a reversal of that trend towards proliferation of things which had taken place during the last days of the *ancien régime*. During the Napoleonic period, only relatively few and essential forms were retained. The wide range of beds in particular was reduced, and beds were simplified.

The Empire style reflected the person of Napoleon himself, in its grandness of conception, combined with its Neoclassical severity of execution. The monumentality of furniture pays homage to Napoleon the emperor, while the greater restraint in the execution of furniture forms is in sympathy with his militarism. When Napoleon was defeated at Waterloo in 1815, the collapse of his empire also marked the end of the style which had characterized it. Although the Empire style did not entirely disappear, the quality of craftsmanship declined swiftly, as the inspiration was no longer there.

England

The emergence of the Neoclassical style in England coincided with the accession of King George III in 1760. The preceding Rococo style had only managed to sustain and amuse its patrons for a short time in England, having reached its apogee during the course of the 1750s. Rococo's decline in the 1760s was fairly swift in the face of the rising popularity of Neoclassicism. George III's reign was a long one, spanning almost the entire length of the Neoclassical period in England. But although the era of Neoclassicism coincided with the reign of George III, it is not generally associated with his name. Rather, it is the great architects and designers of the period whose names are used to describe its early phases—the architect-designer Robert Adam (1728–92), and the furniture designers George Hepplewhite (d. 1786) and Thomas Sheraton (c. 1751–1806). The last and most prolonged period of George III's reign, the one during the course of which he went mad, is associated with his son, later George IV, who from the time of his coming of age in 1783 to the time of his death in 1830 was one of the outstanding, albeit unpopular, patrons of his time. Although he acted as prince regent only for the years between 1811 and 1820, the style now labelled Regency extended beyond the official years of his term of office to encompass the first thirty years of the nineteenth century.

ABOVE *This harp, which was made by the Parisian lute-makers 'Cousieau, father and son', for the Empress Joséphine's Music Room at Malmaison, was probably the one played by Hortense Beauharnais who excelled at both harp and piano. Hortense was one of Joséphine's children by her first marriage to the Vicomte Alexandre de Beauharnais. The Imperial eagle sits proudly on top of the harp.*

LEFT   The tapestry room at Osterley Park is one of the most brilliantly coloured rooms designed by the Scottish architect–designer Robert Adam. Adam was often personally responsible for the design of every detail in a room. Ceiling designs were reflected in carpets, wall-hangings matched upholstery, and motifs were repeated on friezes, cornices, door handles and furniture. These famous deep-rose pink tapestries were specially woven in France, in 1775. This room acts as an ante-chamber to the state bedchamber.

RIGHT   A marquetry commode and matching pair of pedestals by John Cobb. Despite their elaborate Rococo bombé forms these pieces are Neoclassical in their marquetry decoration, and they incorporate swags of husks, oval medallions, vases of flowers and honeysuckle. The pedestals were probably originally intended to be candlestands and the elegant urn-shaped marble vases were added shortly after their completion. The mirror was made to a design by Adam in 1772 and is in a more rectilinear form.

Neoclassicism was cautiously welcomed in England from the beginning of the 1760s. Thomas Chippendale included a few plates in the 'new' style in his *Director*, when he reissued it in 1762 and James 'Athenian' Stuart's and Nicholas Revett's *The Antiquities of Athens* appeared in the same year. But it was not until after the Seven Years War and the resumption of Anglo-French relations in 1763 that the Neoclassical style really became established in England. Paris was already in the grip of the *goût grècque* and this must have delighted the English aristocrats to whom Parisian society once again extended hospitality. But it was a young, relatively unknown architect, Robert Adam, who was to provide the greatest impetus for the development of the Neoclassical style in England. His fertile imagination, his abounding ambition and his outstanding ability enabled him to virtually dictate the direction design would take in England for the next twenty years.

The grand tour was designed to further the general education of young men of means. But for Robert Adam it was a golden opportunity to examine the archaeological discoveries then being made in Italy and Greece. Although he never managed to reach Greece, he was able to go to

FAR LEFT *This candlestand, designed by Adam in about 1770, is in the form of an athénienne or perfume burner. Such pedestals were also used to display Neoclassical busts.*

LEFT *An armchair made in 1764 by Thomas Chippendale to a design by Robert Adam. The chair represents an important development in Adam's early Neoclassical style and is, as Chippendale described it, 'exceedingly richly carved in the Antick manner'.*

BELOW *A magnificent marquetry commode made, and probably designed, by Chippendale for Harewood House, at a cost of £86. It includes a dressing-table drawer in the centre and is luxuriously veneered in satinwood.*

several important sites including the Palace of Diocletian at Split (Spalato) and Herculaneum. He was aided by the French architect and draftsman, Charles Clerisseau, who after their meeting in Florence had agreed to give the young Adam lessons. Adam wrote jubilantly to his younger brother James:

> I found out Clerisseau, a Nathaniel in whom tho' there is no guile, Yet there is the utmost knowledge of Architecture, of perspective & of Designing & Colouring I ever Saw, or had any Conception of; He rais'd my Ideas, He created emulation and fire in my Brest. I wish'd above all things to learn his manner . . .

Clerisseau was himself steeped in the excitement and fervour of Neoclassicism. He led Adam around the monuments and buildings of ancient Rome, and introduced him to the many authorities on the Neoclassical movement then staying in the city.

Rome in 1755 was a fascinating place. It was a centre for all those interested in the arts and culture, particularly the classical arts of ancient Rome, which had their source in the city itself. Men of great intellectual, cultural and artistic distinction from all over Europe were drawn there— collectors such as Sir William Hamilton (whose collection of Etruscan vases was bought by the British Museum in 1772), theorists like the German, Winckelmann, and painters such as Piranesi, whom Adam described as the only Italian to 'breathe the Ancient Air'.

The tour proved to be an experience of inestimable value to Adam, who continued to reap the benefit thereof for the rest of his life. Not only did

RIGHT *On his return from the grand tour in 1758, Robert Adam quickly received a number of commissions from wealthy and fashionable patrons. This is the state dining room at Kedleston Hall, home of the first Baron Scarsdale, which Adam designed in 1761. His use of a semi-domed apsidal end to the room provided a focal point for the suite of sideboard furniture which Adam also designed.*

his knowledge of Rome inspire him to 'transfuse the beautiful spirit of antiquity with novelty and variety', but his tireless efforts to record all that he saw while in Italy provided him with a vocabulary so extensive in its scope that he was able to draw upon it constantly from the time of his return in 1758 to his death in 1792, and other designers continued to be inspired by his findings for a long time after his death. There were only two other Neoclassical designers of importance, William Chambers, who had also studied in Italy, and James 'Athenian' Stuart, who had travelled to Greece, and had in the 1750s been responsible for the first Neoclassical decorations in England, in the interior of Spencer House.

Adam's enormous success in London after his return was truly remarkable. Within only a few years, his practice became the most fashionable in England. Although each was important, Adam worked on relatively few commissions, but they were often simultaneous, which led him to complain that he was 'with difficulty able to get Managed with Honour to myself & Satisfaction to my Employers'. But that he did somehow manage is evidenced by such magnificent edifices as Syon House, Osterley Park, Kedleston Hall, Nostell Priory, and many others.

Adam not only popularized a number of new decorative motifs, he also influenced form and interior designs. Where generally the Neoclassicism of Adam differed from that of the Palladians twenty years earlier was in his lighter and more decorative use of ornament and forms. In this he was to some extent influenced by the delicacy and freedom of Rococo decoration. Furthermore, although like Kent before him he was faced with the problem of finding suitable ancient prototypes for furniture designs, he had the advantage of the increased archaeological knowledge which had built up during the course of the intervening years, which had been made generally available through publications such as those of Piranesi's meticulously drawn copies of ancient Roman originals. Adam's earliest works show that he was prepared to experiment with the new forms and decorations in order to achieve a style which suited him. These pieces are often heavy and curvilinear in outline, showing the influence of both Palladian and Rococo pieces. But they were new in that the type of ornament which he grafted on to such frames was Neoclassical in inspiration. Gradually, through experimentation with different forms, Adam developed his own idiosyncratic style of Neoclassicism. He increasingly rejected the heavy, massive style of the Palladians in favour of a lighter, more linear and graceful style, which in its maturity achieved an elegance rarely surpassed. Adam's repertoire of Classical ornaments included rams' heads and anthemions, paterae and sphinxes, as well as festoons of corn husks or bell-shaped flowers, which he often used to link together dominant motifs or themes on pieces of furniture. He used these patterns and ornaments to emphasize and enhance the overall form.

RIGHT   *An imposing mahogany 'commode clothes-press' made and supplied to Sir Rowland Winn of Nostell Priory by Thomas Chippendale. The invoice, dated 22 June 1767, describes it as being of 'exceedingly fine wood in a commode shape with 7 shelves in the upper part lind with paper & green bays aprons, and 4 drawers in the under part with best wrought handles to ditto'. The account for £37.00 made this a very expensive piece of furniture in its time but the superb quality of the mahogany, the design and execution amply justified its considerable expense.*

The impact of Adam's stylistic innovations exerted a profound influence on furniture styles of the period. Within a few years every furniture-maker of note was offering furniture designed in the new style. Wealthy clients enjoyed opportunities to examine new pieces in the fashionable shops which dotted London, from Soho to Berkeley Square, including pieces by makers of the calibre of Thomas Chippendale and John Linnell, who supplied furniture in the new style to several important houses.

During the course of the 1760s and 1770s Adam's supremacy as a designer remained unquestioned. But gradually towards the last quarter of the eighteenth century there was a decline in the number of important commissions available, due partly to the economic cutbacks made necessary by the American Revolution which began in 1776. The dearth of publications during the third quarter of the eighteenth century meant that Adam produced almost the only set of furniture designs, many of which were for specific commissions.

LEFT *A mahogany dressing table made by Thomas Chippendale and supplied to Nostell Priory in 1769. Although the ornamental detailing, such as the paterae and fluting is thoroughly Neoclassical, the form is similar to some designs in the* Director, *first published in 1754. The slightly concave doors conceal a cupboard in which was kept an 'enameld China basin and Bottle' and the dressing drawer is fitted with a mirror, assorted compartments and 'conveniences for shaving'.*

ABOVE *A dining room suite, consisting of sideboard-table, wine-cooler, and a pair of flanking pedestals made by Thomas Chippendale in about 1772. It demonstrates Chippendale's remarkable facility for absorbing Adam's full Neoclassical style. These items of dining-room furniture were among Robert Adam's most important innovations and were widely imitated by other designers and furniture-makers. Veneered in rosewood with tulipwood bandings, this set is decorated with ormolu mounts of a very high quality.*

The appearance in 1769 of the *New Book of Pier Frames* (wall furniture), by Mathias Lock was hardly a threat to the thriving practice of Robert Adam and his brother James. But George Hepplewhite's *The Cabinet Maker and Upholsterer's Guide*, published in 1788, two years after his death, was aimed at a wider market, and helped disseminate the fashions already introduced by Adam and several leading furniture-makers to a much wider clientèle. Hepplewhite's name has been used to describe the predominant style of that time, although his work was far less innovative and imaginative than that of either his predecessor Adam, or of his successor Thomas Sheraton. Indeed, it was not Hepplewhite's aim to create new furniture styles. His great achievement was to create designs for a far wider range of furniture than Adam had ever done, and many of his designs were for more ordinary furniture, which Adam had not concerned himself with. Thus Hepplewhite made fashionable certain forms of furniture which have subsequently become associated solely with his name, like the distinctive forms used on chair backs such as shield, heart and oval shapes (although the latter were frequently used by Adam).

In England as in France, there was an increase in the variety and number of small pieces of furniture, especially delicate, light and moveable items like tables. One such was the Pembroke table thought by Hepplewhite to be of 'considerable elegance', which in form was similar to the breakfast table illustrated by Chippendale. In design, the table was small, light and attractively decorated, generally with marquetry or painted floral decorations. The small flaps on either side of its rectangular or oval form could be raised and supported by hinged brackets underneath, thus increasing the overall size of the table's surface. Straight, tapering legs were generally shown in Hepplewhite's designs, although occasional references to Rococo cabriole forms were used.

Japanning was increasingly used on furniture, since the revival of marquetry, popular since the beginning of the Neoclassical style, was proving to be expensive. Light, elegant woods, particularly flashing, golden satinwood, replaced the darker tones of mahogany.

French Neoclassical influences, apparent even in Adam's designs, became more prominent during the 1780s as many French émigrés fled to England before the Revolution. French forms and terms, such as the *bonheur du jour* (small writing and dressing table), the *duchesse* and the

LEFT *Elegantly designed Pembroke tables were much sought after in the late eighteenth century. They were a simplified form of the breakfast table illustrated in Chippendale's* Director, *and while a few retained a tray below, they generally consisted of a table with two flaps and a centre drawer. Their small size and the addition of brass casters made them light and easy to move. They are probably named after the Countess of Pembroke who, according to Sheraton, 'first gave order for one of them, and who probably gave the first idea of such a table to the workmen'.*

ABOVE *A japanned commode in the rectilinear Neoclassical style developed by Robert Adam. Made for Harewood House by Thomas Chippendale in about 1771, it continues the long-established fashion for lacquered furniture, popular since the time of the Restoration in the middle of the seventeenth century.*

confidante (sofa) became as familiar to the *beau monde* of London as they were to the French aristocracy.

The Cabinet Maker and Upholsterer's Guide was the largest and most comprehensive pattern book to appear since Chippendale's *Director* in 1754. It must have been enormously popular with the lesser firms of furniture-makers who were endeavouring to meet the demands of an increasingly fashion-conscious clientèle, and its designs for simple, elegant pieces were republished the following year and again in 1794. Although Hepplewhite may be regarded as having achieved what he set out to achieve, namely, 'to unite elegance and utility, and blend the useful with the agreeable', many of his designs, had 'caught the decline', or so, at any rate, said the astute, competitive Sheraton. Be that as it may, Hepplewhite's designs were enormously successful, and stimulated the publication of other pattern books, such as Thomas Shearer's *Cabinet-Maker's London Book of Prices* (1788), and Sheraton's own *The Cabinet-Maker and Upholsterer's Drawing Book*.

As Hepplewhite's *Guide* typifies the fashions of the 1780s, so Sheraton's *Drawing Book*, brought out between 1791 and 1794, is representative of

RIGHT *The magnificent state bed designed by Robert Adam for Osterley Park in the autumn of 1776 as part of an overall scheme, which included a set of six armchairs, one of which is illustrated below.*

the fashions of its decade. Like the *Guide*, the *Drawing Book* was aimed at a wide market, to meet demand at home and abroad, and was similar to the *Guide* in its stress on elegance and simplicity. Sheraton's main innovation was to replace the curvilinear oval forms favoured by Hepplewhite with rectilinear forms. Sheraton's decorations also tended to be simpler. He replaced the Neoclassical paterae, husks and urns of Adam and Hepplewhite with geometric inlay. But though Sheraton's ornamentation generally tended to be simpler than that of Hepplewhite, he sometimes went to the other extreme. Flamboyantly naturalistic painted decorations often featured in his designs, and he also introduced kidney shapes, domes and tambours. Near the end of his life, in fact, Sheraton published some designs so fantastic that their execution would not have been possible.

ABOVE RIGHT *Sofa-tables were essential items in the more informal arrangement of early nineteenth-century household interiors. This rosewood example was made by Thomas Chippendale the Younger for Sir Richard Colt Hoare of Stourhead.*

BELOW RIGHT *This serpentine-shaped chest of drawers with cupboards on either side is veneered with finely figured satinwood.*

The chaotic situation in France before, during, and for some time after the Revolution had a salutary effect on other European countries. London absorbed many members of the exiled French aristocracy. The influx of émigré furniture-makers meant that English designers and furniture-makers became more and more familiar with their work. *Marchands-merciers*, such as Daguerre, also came. They supplied quantities of fine French furniture to several houses in England, including the Prince of Wales' new London residence, Carlton House, which was designed by the architect Henry Holland. Holland's work was distinguished by an extreme simplicity verging on austerity, which anticipated the future Empire style. Much of Holland's work was based on classical and Egyptian designs, and his assistant, Tathum, who was living in Italy (at Holland's expense) was able to furnish him with a constant supply of these designs. It was probably Holland who inspired Sheraton to include in his last two publications several designs which reflected the new trend towards a stricter, more literal interpretation of classical designs.

But it was actually the publication in 1807 of Thomas Hope's book, *Household Furniture and Interior Decoration*, which signalled the emergence of a serious interest in rediscovering and reviving the 'pure spirit of classical antiquity' (as opposed to its more superficial attributes). Thomas Hope was a wealthy connoisseur who decorated his house in Duchess Street in a thoroughly 'antique' manner. The main reception rooms, situated on the first floor, were especially designed to accommodate his wide collection of Greek, Roman and Egyptian remains. Interiors and furniture were designed to harmonize with these splendid artifacts. Hope's house, in its historical verisimilitude, was imitated by many admirers of true antiquity, even before Hope's book about it was published. His book did not have the same aim as previous design books by Chippendale, Hepplewhite, and Sheraton. Indeed, it was not so much a pattern book as a visual statement. But it did have considerable impact on English taste. Motifs such as ringed lions' masks and finely carved lions' paw feet, which had previously appeared only occasionally on furniture, were suddenly very popular. Hope's designs were made more generally available, and imitable, with the appearance, in 1808, of another book, *Collection of Designs for Household Furniture and Interior Decoration*, by George Smith. While Hope's book was written to describe, rather than to instruct, Smith's book was intended to do both, and it included a wide variety of domestic furniture.

In the early nineteenth century, classical artifacts which had been unearthed through archaeological explorations were widely used as models. Stools, popular in ancient times, become fashionable during the Regency period, and were frequently decorated with outsplayed legs in the form of sabres. The ancient Greek form of chair, the klismos chair,

was modified to become a much-used model for the chair with tablet-shaped back rail. The rail extended over the end of its supports and gave the chair a distinctive horizontal emphasis. Such a surface provided a marvellous area for decoration, usually with an imitation of ancient vase painting. Sofas for lounging upon were made in the form of ancient Greek sofas. Pembroke tables, which had been among the most graceful and elegant pieces of furniture in late eighteenth-century drawing rooms, were transformed into sofa-tables. They retained the flaps at the ends, but were elongated. Early examples show elegantly shaped end supports, but gradually these become heavier. Large surface areas, particularly on case furniture, were left unadorned, but legs became increasingly sculptural. Splendidly carved monopodia, in the forms of lions and winged sphinxes, were, in their heroic proportions, examples of Regency furniture's increasing tendency towards monumentality.

To meet the growing demands of a rapidly expanding population, a trend towards mass production began around 1800. The simple outlines and austerely plain surfaces, decorated only with limited areas of applied bronze motifs, which Hope had introduced, were eminently adaptable to the techniques of mass production. Decoration in the form of inlay also came back into fashion in the early part of the century. Early examples of inlay show ebony stringing-lines, but after about 1810 brass inlay became popular again, as the vogue for Boulle work returned. The bright warm tones of brass, in floral or linear patterns, reflected well against the darker hues of woods such as rosewood and mahogany which had replaced, in popularity, the lighter-coloured woods used at the turn of the

century. Gilding was widely used, and was particularly striking on new forms of furniture, such as the distinctive circular convex-shaped mirrors.

During the Regency period, novelty was of primary importance in matters of taste. The Neoclassical style which predominated was constantly in a state of flux to accommodate the new ideas arriving from France, and deriving from discoveries in Greece, Rome and Egypt. At the same time, more romantic styles, such as chinoiserie and Gothick, which had never completely died out during the eighteenth century, were revived. The Prince Regent, who was a well-known leader of fashion, paved the way for a revival of romantic orientalism with the flamboyantly exotic pavilion which he had built at Brighton. As early as 1807, Smith had introduced Gothick designs in his *Collections* and was to include many more in his later book, *The Cabinet Maker and Upholsterer's Guide*, brought out in 1828. The more florid designs in this book reflected the general tendency of later Regency furniture. After around 1815, forms became less elegant and even coarse. Ornament became opulent. The sculptural quality that had distinguished earlier Regency furniture became exaggerated, and scrolling forms and volutes reappeared. Legs, which in the early days of the Regency period had been elegantly and gracefully curved or tapered, now became stumpy and bulbous, anticipating the ponderous fashions of the early Victorian period.

ABOVE LEFT *The increasing search for novelty in furniture design during the early nineteenth century led some designers, such as Sheraton, to produce more and more fantastic designs. But these chairs, made by Chippendale the Younger in 1812, are of a surprisingly restrained design.*

ABOVE RIGHT *A leading antiquarian in the early nineteenth century was the wealthy connoisseur, Thomas Hope. This chair, made to his design, illustrates the wide knowledge of ancient Greek and Egyptian forms which he acquired during his extensive travels. Made for the Egyptian room of his London house, it is decorated with Egyptian figures.*

The Low Countries

The strength of French and English influences on furniture design in the Netherlands in the eighteenth century ensured the introduction of Neoclassicism into Holland by the 1770s. Indeed, French and English influence was so strong that it was more fashionable to import pieces made by famous Parisian and London furniture-makers than it was to commission work from local makers. This was very damaging to the development of Dutch cabinet-making, which had steadily deteriorated during the course of the century. In 1771, the powerful Joseph Guild of Amsterdam took steps to prohibit any further imports of foreign furniture, in order to protect the home industry. This did help to promote Dutch furniture, and Dutch furniture-making improved as a result. But

RIGHT *Chamfered corners and solid, short, tapering legs are typical features of eighteenth-century Dutch case furniture. This example, executed in a variety of woods, is in the form of a commode and would probably be used in a drawing room. The hinged top is shown open and the two flaps which encircle the recessed basin can also be pulled open. Known as an* opflagtafel *this type of serving-table was used to display glasses, which could then be rinsed before or after use in the small basin.*

French and English Neoclassical tastes were so influential that they continued to dominate Netherlandish fashions throughout the period.

As elsewhere in Europe, furniture in the Netherlands became generally more rectilinear in form and outline. Commodes, bureaux and cupboards were no longer made with extravagant *bombé* or serpentine shapes. New forms, such as the *secrétaire à abattant*, were introduced from France. English trends were evident particularly in the increasing use of mahogany for the frames of chairs, and of mahogany veneers.

But despite the Anglo-French influences, a number of Netherlandish characteristics did remain on Neoclassical furniture. Marquetry decoration, important in the Dutch tradition, continued to be used on a number of items, such as commodes, cupboards, and tables. Dutch marquetry decoration was distinguished by the wide bands of veneer often used to frame a central panel of pictorial marquetry. Lacquer decoration, too, which Holland had been so instrumental in popularizing during the seventeenth century, was widely used in the form of decorative panels during the last quarter of the century. Inlay, generally of a geometric pattern, was another distinctive feature of Netherlandish furniture, which, like the sharply tapered leg also favoured, bears more similarity to contemporary Italian furniture decoration than to French styles. The tendency, seen throughout the eighteenth century in the Netherlands, to chamfer the corners of case furniture, continued during the Neoclassical period.

By the last quarter of the century, the Netherlands were shattered politically and economically. Defeated first by the English, in 1784, the Netherlands were overrun and defeated yet again by Napoleon's armies in 1795. Napoleon promptly abolished many institutions, including the powerful guild system. French domination was sealed with the creation of a puppet monarchy, and King Louis Napoleon and Queen Hortense were crowned amidst great ceremony in 1806.

The Empire style, introduced into the Netherlands at the beginning of the nineteenth century, was used to great effect when the old town hall in Amsterdam was converted into a royal palace for the new monarchs. The new palace was reconstructed and equipped mainly by local Dutch craftsmen, though one important cabinet-maker, Carel Breytspraak, was of German origin. Percier and Fontaine, two of Napoleon's own designers, had promoted the new style throughout the Empire through their publications. The style, severely rectilinear and spare in its decoration, brought a return to favour of sombre, dark woods, such as mahogany and rosewood. Decoration was mostly in the form of ormolu mounts, though these were used more sparingly than in France. A distinctive feature of Breytspraak's work was his technique of framing decorative panels of highly grained veneer by recessing them into the furniture.

LEFT *The exuberance of the carved decoration on this elaborate writing cabinet is typical of Italian furniture-making in the eighteenth century. It was made by Giuseppe-Maria Bonzanigo in about 1780 and may have been intended to celebrate the marriage between a prince of the royal house of Savoy and a princess of France.*

The impact of the Empire style in the Netherlands was so great that it continued, as in Italy, to be fashionable for a long time after Napoleon's downfall in 1815. But while the classical lines of the Empire style were retained, the overtones of Imperialism gradually disappeared, to be replaced by a homely elegance and simplicity more akin to the German Biedermeier style.

Italy

During the course of the nineteenth century, there was, throughout Europe, an increasing interest in Italy's ancient heritage. A number of important archaeological discoveries were made there, including those of Herculaneum and Pompeii. Although relatively few Italians took part in these archaeological expeditions, the constant thronging of foreigners to Italy, and particularly to Rome, made Italy once again the intellectual and artistic centre of Europe.

The painter-designer who exerted the major influence on Italian Neoclassicism (and indeed, who strongly influenced Neoclassicism throughout Europe) was Giovanni Baptiste Piranesi (1720–78), a Venetian. Piranesi was the staunchest and most persuasive advocate of the Roman cause in the prolonged battle of artists, academics and connoisseurs over the relative virtues of Roman and Greek antiquities. Piranesi's eloquence lay more in his works than in his words, and his romantic vision of Rome's ancient glories was embodied in a constant outpouring of exquisite illustrations. His interest in archaeology dated back to the time when, as a student in Rome, he had first come across antiquities. In 1769, Piranesi published his *Diverse Maniere d'ardonare i Camini*, in which he included several designs for tables, vases and candelabra, based on his own extensive studies of ancient artifacts.

But despite the fact that Rome was the international centre of Neoclassicism, and that Piranesi propagated the new style, it did not really establish itself in Italy until the last quarter of the century, although new museums and academic centres were being established, from Milan in the North to Naples in the south, which did help to promote Neoclassicism. In Milan, an academy was started in 1755 under the direction of the eminent Neoclassicist, Giocondo Albertolli, and within a few years, some furniture there was reflecting the new style.

Neoclassicism never met with country-wide enthusiasm in Italy. A few centres, notably Venice, were barely affected by it, preferring Baroque and Rococo styles. Elsewhere, however, Rococo scrolls gave way to Neoclassical ornamentation, and Rococo curves to more architectural, rectilinear forms. The designs of Hepplewhite and Sheraton had some influence in Italy, but only minor cabinet-makers, whose names are unknown, followed the English examples, and they were employed only to decorate the smaller houses – that is, the houses of middle-class patrons, rather than the palaces of the aristocracy. The French Louis XVI style was favoured by the aristocrats and the newly rich, so it was this style which had the greatest apparent influence on Italian Neoclassical furniture. But whether modelled on the furniture designs of England or of France, generally speaking, Italian furniture could not be compared to the furniture of those countries, for Italian workmanship at that time was far inferior.

Milan, the capital of Lombardy, which was still under the benign rule of Austria, was noted particularly as the centre for the best marquetry work in Italy. This was due mainly to the presence there of one of the finest marqueteurs of the time, Giuseppe Maggiolini (d. 1814). He was appointed court *intarsiatore* (intarsia being the traditional form of inlay work used in Italy since the time of the Renaissance), to the Governor General of Lombardy, the Archduke Ferdinand, under whose auspices Maggiolini had received his early training. Maggiolini's style is distinguished by a restrained elegance which reflects the Louis XVI style. Like Piffetti earlier in the century, Maggiolini was one of the few Italian furniture-makers who could truly be called an *ébéniste*. His commodes are particularly noteworthy for their fine simplicity, their rectilinear outlines enlivened only by striking marquetry panels of Neoclassical design.

In Turin, the most famous craftsman was Giuseppe Maria Bonzanigo, who worked in the Italian tradition of elaborate wood-carving. Sculptural carving also remained popular further south in Rome. Rome was still noted for its monumental furniture, which, though often inspired by antique pieces even then being excavated from the surrounding country-side, still owed as much to Baroque ideas as to Neoclassical models. A bronze table cast by Giuseppe Valadier for the Vatican in 1789 bears striking witness to the sculptural Baroque quality of Rome's Neo-classicism.

The collapse of the Bourbon dynasty in France after the Revolution had led to the demise of the Louis XVI style of Neoclassicism in France, and paved the way for the Empire style. The Empire style was quickly established in Italy, as elsewhere, during the first decade of the nineteenth century, in the wake of Napoleon's successful campaigns there. The result was an increasing academicism in furniture design, and closer imitation of classical form and ornament.

Milan, now under French instead of Austrian rule, remained an import-ant artistic centre, under the patronage of its new Viceroy, Prince Eugene Beauharnais. Other important centres were Naples, where Napoleon's sister Caroline reigned with her husband, and Rome, where Napoleon's

BELOW *Despite the variety of the carved and gilded decoration used on this stool, the grandeur of the design and the richness of its upholstery recall the Imperial overtones of the International Empire style which continued to be popular in Italy well into the 1830s. Made in about 1835 after a design by Pelagio Palagi, this stool was part of a suite of furniture destined for the Palazzo Reale, Turin.*

sister Pauline became a princess of the powerful Borghese family. Pauline, with the help of the French Ambassador Joseph Bonaparte, succeeded in introducing into Rome not only French designs for furniture, but also the French language, and French dress.

Venice remained virtually untouched by the new Napoleonic fashions, and for a time suffered an almost total cultural eclipse, due to the near collapse of her economy.

Since Italian furniture-making tended to be inferior in craftsmanship to French, much of the new Empire-style furniture was either imported from France or made by French craftsmen, who were encouraged to establish themselves in Italy so that they could supply furniture to the various palaces of the Napoleonic dynasty. But symbols of Napoleon's

BELOW *A writing table made in the internationally famous workshop of David Roentgen. French influences are clearly apparent in the light, elegant design of the piece. At the touch of several carefully concealed springs innumerable drawers fly open.*

martial victories were not used on Italian furniture, as they were on French. Instead, traditional Italian painted decoration was widely employed on Empire pieces. Antique models, like the Greek klismos chair and the Roman curule (chair) were much imitated in Italian Empire furniture design.

The French Empire collapsed in 1815, and the Italian princes returned to their country and their thrones. The newly restored monarchs were so delighted by the Empire style which they found upon their return, that, instead of banishing all vestiges of Napoleon's rule, they continued to cultivate the style. Indeed, one prince is reputed to have said, 'If only we had been away for another ten years!' Thus, for several years after the collapse of the Empire style elsewhere in Europe, it continued as the official style in Italy, though gradually, during the course of the nineteenth century, more typically Italian carving once again superseded the austerely linear Empire forms.

Germany and Austria

Many of the German courts and furniture-making centres in the last quarter of the eighteenth century were reluctant to abandon Rococo flamboyance for the more attenuated elegance of early Neoclassicism. It was not until the 1780s that the new style, already well established elsewhere in Europe, was finally taken up in Germany. Neoclassical forms there were modelled on predominantly French and English contemporary forms. A new repertoire of ornamentation, including festoons of flowers, rams' heads, anthemions and classical urns replaced the more vivacious ornaments of the preceding Rococo style.

BELOW   This bed was made for Queen Luise and is still in the Charlottenburg Palace, Berlin. Decoration is minimal compared to contemporary French and English pieces. The pale golden colour of the bed, veneered in pearwood, combined with the clean elegant lines anticipates the simple homely appeal of Biedermeier furniture.

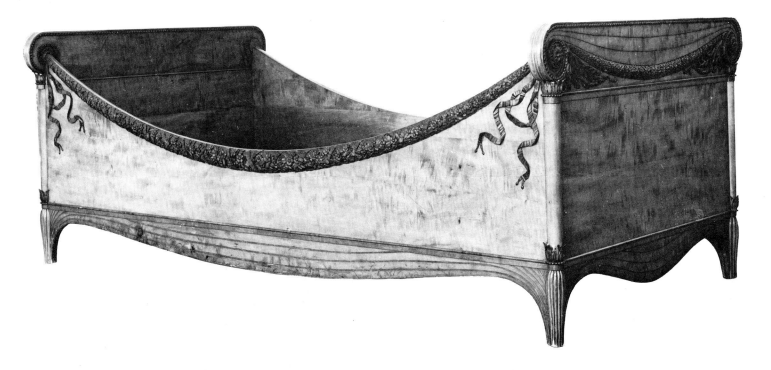

The most important figure to emerge in Germany at this time was David Roentgen (1743–1807), who had taken over his father's workshop in 1771. Roentgen, widely travelled and well educated, achieved even greater fame than his father, Abraham, and is regarded as one of the finest of all German cabinet-makers. As a young man in Paris, he quickly gained himself an international reputation and worked subsequently for several royal courts in Europe, from Russia to England. His finest work was for Marie Antoinette, queen of Louis XVI, who was noted for the number of German cabinet-makers she employed, including also Beneman and Weisweiller. Roentgen was admired not only for his superb cabinet work and fine marquetry decoration, often executed to the designs of Januarius Zick, but also for the ingenious mechanical furniture which he devised for his wealthy clients. After he returned to his father's workshop in Germany, he continued to send furniture to his princely patrons, and many of his pieces are distinguished by the way they can be broken down into different sections. Legs on tables, for instance, invariably unscrew, making travel very much safer. Roentgen's work was in advance of other German furniture-makers; by the 1780s his style became highly tectonic, and the severe outlines and plain veneers of his furniture anticipated the approaching Empire style. Although he worked primarily for the various royal courts of Europe, he was instrumental in helping to propagate the Neoclassical style in Germany in the late eighteenth and early nineteenth centuries.

The widespread successes of the French Revolutionary forces in the 1790s and the rapid elevation of their brilliant general, Napoleon Bonaparte, self-appointed emperor after the turn of the century, caused the new Empire style to spread rapidly throughout Europe. By 1803, Napoleon's army had conquered Germany up to the Rhineland and within two years he had successfully crushed any vestige of Austrian opposition. His occupation of Vienna marked the end of the once mighty Holy Roman Empire. Prussia, the last important territory in Central Europe to withstand the French onslaught, fell in 1806 and for a decade Germany, now drastically simplified under Napoleon's reorganization, remained under the dominant influence of France.

The Napoleonic wars had left a widespread legacy of poverty in Germany. But notwithstanding this, several courts, particularly in southern and central Germany (where some, like Württemburg and Bavaria, had been elevated to royal status) undertook elaborate rebuilding and refurnishing schemes. Roentgen provided several magnificent pieces for the Prussian court while Johann Valentin Raab, working for the court at Würzburg between 1808 and 1812, was responsible for making several pieces in the new Empire style, although they were characteristically less severe than the examples made in Paris.

ABOVE *A simple uncluttered appearance makes this interior by Johann Erdmann Hummel typical of the restrained Biedermeier style that was particularly popular with the middle classes in Germany during the early nineteenth century.*

RIGHT *A pair of elaborate gilded chairs of state made for the Queen's throne room in the Munich Residenz to a design by the head of the Bavarian State Building Authority Louis von Klenz.*

In Austria, Vienna, with its predominantly middle-class rather than aristocratic society, was the furniture-making centre which was least affected by the Empire style. A much less formal style was evident in the work of cabinet-makers such as Johann Haertl whose simple forms anticipated the later Biedermeier style. Typical of Haertl's work were the curious elliptical forms which he used, particularly on writing furniture, and the lyre motif which he often introduced into his designs. Other cabinet-makers working in Vienna were Ernest Seiffert, Martin Schacker and Johann Reimann.

The development of the German Confederation, formed after the Congress of Vienna in 1814, coincided with the development of a style which lasted into the 1830s. This style, subsequently known as the Biedermeier style, was the most important development in Germany at this time. The Biedermeier style originated in Vienna. It quickly became a national Austrian style, and then spread throughout Germany, though the royal courts of Munich and Berlin remained almost untouched by it. 'Biedermeier', like Baroque, was coined initially as a derogatory term. It was based on the caricature figure of 'Papa Biedermeier' who was then a comic symbol of middle-class values. Papa Biedermeier represented comfort and respectability. At this time in Germany, particular emphasis was placed on family and domestic life, and on private activities such as letter-writing. The Biedermeier furniture associated with letter-writing was extremely popular. Despite its rejection of the earlier Empire style, with its imperial overtones, the new Biedermeier style had its roots in both the Empire and the Louis XVI styles. While retaining the simple outlines of the former, the Biedermeier style revived the less didactic motifs of the latter. The dark heavy woods of the Empire style were generally replaced by lighter-coloured woods, particularly native woods such as elm and fruitwoods.

In Munich the extensive building programmes in progress both during and after the fall of the Empire were strongly influenced by the crown prince, later crowned Ludwig I in 1825, who was an advocate of Neo-classicism. The Court Architect Leo von Klenze, himself influenced by Empire designers such as Percier and Fontaine, maintained the Neo-classical tradition. His buildings and their furniture, some of which he designed, were as appropriate to this monarchically inclined city as Biedermeier was to the middle-class capital of Vienna.

Similar architectural tendencies could be seen in the Prussian capital of Berlin, where the Court Architect Karl Friedrich Schinkel maintained a Neoclassical style. But in furniture design, Schinkel introduced his own style of Biedermeier, based on the forms of Roman antiquity. Its functional, clean outlines and sparing use of decoration foreshadowed later modern trends. Berlin was famous for the quality and elegance of its

NEAR RIGHT *Side chairs were generally made in fairly large sets, although with the passage of time many of these sets were divided and individual pieces were dispersed. This painted example is based fairly closely on a Hepplewhite design and was probably made during the 1790s.*

FAR RIGHT *Despite a number of old-fashioned features, such as the elaborately shaped bracket feet and the intricately carved and pierced pediment, this elegant secrétaire was made at about the turn of the century. The inlaid decoration of the eagle, the fan motifs and the geometric patterned stringing lines are typical of the Federal style and illustrate the high level of craftsmanship achieved by many American makers by the end of the eighteenth century.*

BELOW RIGHT *American Chippendale designs remained popular long after the Neoclassical Federal style had been introduced, as this mahogany secrétaire shows. Despite its outmoded appearance the piece was probably made at the end of the eighteenth century by the Annapolis furniture-maker John Shaw. A distinctive feature of his work was the use of inlaid oval panels.*

furniture and much of it was exported. Among Berlin's most famous cabinet-makers was Karl George Wanschaff (1775–1848) who, in 1825, was responsible for equipping the Sommerhaus at Charlottenburg Park. Shortly after this he was appointed Court Cabinet-maker.

Both the Empire and the Biedermeier styles continued concurrently into the 1830s. From this time onwards, the popularity of various historical revival styles began to supersede Neoclassicism and by the middle of the century Biedermeier simplicity had been replaced by the 'second Rococo'.

North America

The American Revolution (1776–83) temporarily disrupted trade and industry, and links with England were for a time suspended. The Chippendale style continued to be popular, although of course in England it had been superseded by Neoclassicism. America resumed its cultural links with England after the ratification of the Federal Constitution in 1788. While America was no longer dependent on England for trade, England was more than ever seen as the source of inspiration for American decorative arts, particularly in styles of furniture. By the end of the century, furniture-making was one of the most advanced arts in the colonies. In urban communities, specialized workshops had developed, making specific items according to demand, although in rural districts the furniture-maker was still responsible for all the different aspects of his craft. Hepplewhite's and Sheraton's design books arrived in America shortly after their publication in England, thanks to the great improvements which had taken place in communications and travel. The fact that the colonies had been on hostile terms with England during the war years meant that the pure Adam style, which had been so important in England during the 1770s, was not much imitated in America. Furniture-makers were far more influenced by the later leaders of English furniture design, namely Hepplewhite, Shearer and Sheraton. The style of furniture produced in America during the course of the next twenty years coincided with the establishment of the federal government, and thus the Neoclassical period in America is called the Federal period.

Many of the motifs of the Neoclassical style in both England and America had originated with Adam, but had been freely interpreted by the late eighteenth-century London furniture-makers and designers. These motifs included the popular paterae, husks of wheat, pretty and delicate swags of flowers and urns. All of these decorations were as popular in America as they were in England. Following the Declaration of Independence, American cabinet-makers added the newly adopted national emblem, the eagle, to the basic repertoire of classical ornaments. It was displayed on the national flag and on the coinage of the day. On furniture,

RIGHT   *The influence of the French* bonheur du jour *is evident in this elegant lady's cabinet and writing table. Made in about 1800, it features painted oval glass panels decorated with Neoclassical and allegorical figures. Panels painted on the reverse, generally in black and gold, were a speciality of Baltimore furniture-makers during the Federal period.*

the eagle appeared, sometimes carved, sometimes in marquetry work, on a number of important pieces including desks, mirrors and sideboards.

Marquetry was more widely employed during this period than carved ornamentation, such as that used on earlier Rococo pieces. Although America was rich in indigenous woods, American furniture-makers followed the English lead in enthusiastically adopting mahogany as the main wood of the period. Mahogany, regarded by many as the king of woods had been used in America since about 1730, nearly all of it being imported from the West Indies. But due to the difficulties of transportation, it was mainly bought and used by furniture-makers in those areas which were easily accessible to the main shipping points, while inland native woods were used. The availability of a certain type of wood in a particular region sometimes indicates the probable origin of a piece of furniture. While pine and the softer woods were appropriate for use as carcass materials, woods such as maple, cherry and fruitwoods were highly adaptable for decorative veneering work.

Painting, which was less expensive than marquetry or inlay work had for a long time been used as a substitute for marquetry. Adam, in England, had often had furniture painted all over in soft colours to harmonize with his overall design. He had employed painters such as Antonio Zucchi and his wife Angelica Kauffman to paint exquisite pastoral scenes set within delightful idealized backgrounds, on all types of furniture from small chairs to large bookcases. In New York, Adam's influence in this respect was strong. The Hudson River was the source of inspiration for many romantic painters of the nineteenth century. During the Federal period, it was depicted on such pieces as the New York 'fancy' chairs. These chairs were modelled upon chairs in Sheraton's pattern books, and the river views were set within the central panels on the top rails. Painted decoration was also used to simulate inlay and marquetry work, and games-tables, Pembroke tables and chairs were often painted with delightful chains of flowers. In Baltimore an unusual and highly decorative speciality was developed by the brothers John and Hugh Findlay, using glass panels set into furniture. The panels were often decorated on the back with painting, generally in black and gold. This *verre eglomisé* decoration was generally applied in the form of oval or lozenge shaped panels to important pieces, such as desks and sideboards. This type of work was not found in England, and may have originated in a German workshop. Gilding was still not as extensively used as it was in Europe, but was often used to decorate mirror and picture frames and finials, particularly those in the form of eagles.

In the aftermath of the Revolution, there was a shift in the relative importance of various cities. When trade relations with England had been cut off, America had been forced to look elsewhere in order to build up

BELOW *This handsome commode is veneered in a variety of woods, including mahogany, satinwood and rosewood. It was made in 1809 by Thomas Seymour of Boston, for Miss Elizabeth Derby, daughter of Elias Hasket Derby of Salem, one of the wealthiest merchants in New England at the end of the eighteenth century. This commode reflects the influence of the English furniture designer Thomas Sheraton, particularly in the use of the reeded legs.*

LEFT *John Seymour was one of the finest cabinet-makers working in Boston after the Revolution. He was joined by his son in about 1800. This mahogany tambour desk is labelled 'John Seymour & Son, Creek Lane' and was probably made in about 1800. A distinctive feature of Seymour furniture is the duck-egg blue interior.*

ABOVE *This painted armchair is part of a larger set of ten chairs, two settees and a pier-table. The small oval panel on the back contains a painting of a different house belonging to one of Baltimore's most important inhabitants. Three houses depicted which still survive are Montclare, Homewood and Willowbrook. This set is attributed to the workshop of the Findlay brothers.*

her national economy. Even after trade with England was resumed, Americans continued to trade internationally. This expanded trade was of enormous benefit to the new nation, culturally as well as economically. Salem, a town north of Boston which had been a relatively small fishing port, had taken advantage of the booming trade generated by the clipper ships, and had become a commercial and cultural centre during the 1780s. Elias Hasket Derby of Salem was one man who made a fortune through trade, and then became one of America's foremost patrons of the arts. Philadelphia had been the most affluent and creative city during the years immediately before and after the Declaration of Independence. It was then eclipsed by New York, which became the foremost cultural centre when George Washington established himself there during his first term as president.

By the end of the century, the city of New York was the furniture-making centre of the country, from which much furniture was exported

ABOVE   A sideboard of mahogany, one of
a pair made in the workshops of one of
Philadelphia's most fashionable cabinet-
makers, John Aitken. He supplied George
Washington with several pieces of
furniture and was said to be his favourite
cabinet-maker. This piece, made in about
1797, was used by Washington in the
Banqueting Hall at Mount Vernon.
LEFT   This 'masterpiece of Salem' was
made by the cabinet-maker William Lemon
and carved in the Neoclassical style by
Samuel McIntire during the 1790s.
McIntire was recognized as one of the finest
carvers of his day, and he was also a well-
known architect, responsible for designing a
number of buildings in the Federal style in
New England.

RIGHT *Late eighteenth and early nineteenth century American interiors and furniture designs continued to be strongly influenced by English furniture-makers and designers, such as Thomas Sheraton. This furniture, made in fashionable mahogany, is from the extensive workshops of the New York furniture-maker Duncan Phyfe. Phyfe, who owned three large premises in New York, one workshop, one showroom and one warehouse, operated on a scale which foreshadowed the mass production techniques in use by the second quarter of the nineteenth century.*

to the rest of the nation. The most prominent New York cabinet-maker was Duncan Phyfe (1768–1854). As a very young man, Phyfe had immigrated to America with his father, who had set up a furniture-making business in Albany. Phyfe himself stayed in New York City, where he became successful, and by 1815 he owned three properties in the city, which housed not only his workshops, but also a fashionable showroom and a warehouse. Phyfe employed over a hundred men, and his production methods anticipated the assembly-line techniques which were to be used in furniture production later in the century. Although many of Phyfe's designs were derivative, being based on the designs of Hepplewhite and Sheraton, and later on Empire models, he also developed a highly personal style for which he has become famous. He preferred carved ornament to inlay, and this made his work very distinctive at that time. Particularly striking were the fine pieces of table furniture produced in his workshops,

many decorated with carved acanthus leaves on the legs. He was also particularly noted for his use of reed mouldings on the stiles, legs, and arms of chairs.

In Philadelphia, Thomas Affleck and Benjamin Randolph continued to make fine furniture, and Affleck was noted for his Chippendale-style furniture until his death in 1795.

Salem, Massachusetts, was the home of one of America's most fashionable furniture-makers, Samuel McIntire. McIntire was not only a local furniture-maker, he was also the local architect. In contrast to Phyfe, in New York, McIntire was representative of the old-style American cabinet-maker who is responsible for every aspect of a given job. His fame rests on the very fine carved decoration on his furniture. Salem supported at least five other prominent cabinet-makers, all working in the Federal style, including Jacob and Elijah Sanderson, Edmund Johnson, William Hook, and William Lemon.

The Empire style in America began to appear during the first decade of the nineteenth century. It was based on an amalgam of ideas from England and France. The delicate, angular style of the Federal period gave way to a heavier style, and academically 'purer' forms were favoured. By 1810, Phyfe had pioneered the use of the lyre-back chair and sabre legs, and roll-back chairs too had become fashionable. To these Greek and Roman styles were added the Egyptian motifs, popular in France since the late eighteenth century. Several French cabinet-makers, including Charles-Honoré Lannuier and G. J. Lapierre immigrated to New York after the turn of the century, so that the Empire style became quickly established in that city. Smith's pattern book, based on Hope's ideas, was also tremendously popular in America.

Although English pattern books were the major sources of inspiration for American styles, strong regional characteristics persisted into the nineteenth century; for the furniture-making centres along the eastern seaboard, from Charleston, South Carolina to Salem, Massachusetts were as far removed from one another culturally as they were geographically. Though America was now one nation, the variety in the furniture of the period clearly confirms the cosmopolitan character of the country.

LEFT The room used by Marie-Antoinette for her afternoon rest. The restrained decoration of the *boiseries* is typically Neoclassical. Completed in 1781, this was one of a suite of rooms used by the queen.

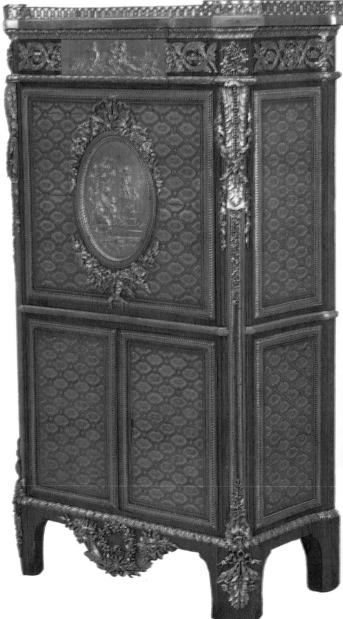

RIGHT This *secrétaire à abattant*, designed to be placed against a wall, has a carcass of oak and is veneered on three sides. The light geometric trellis pattern centres on a water-lily motif. This one was made by J. H. Riesener, but the type of pattern was typical of Oeben, in whose workshop Riesener was trained. The design was a favourite of Marie-Antoinette, to whom the piece was delivered in March 1783.

RIGHT The finely sculpted caryatid, a detail of the commode below, may be by the famous French sculptor, E. M. Falconet, although it has been suggested that it might be by René Dubois himself.

BELOW This commode was the marriage coffer of Marie-Antoinette, wife of Louis XVI, and was probably made by either Jacques Dubois or his son René. René Dubois continued to work with his mother after his father's death and his work was particularly admired by Marie-Antoinette, who in 1779 made him *Ebéniste de la Reine*. The panel in the front, overlaid with gilt bronze fret pattern, is of Japanese lacquer, which continued to be used in furniture during the Neoclassical period.

LEFT A simple mahogany armchair, made in about 1800. The solid tablet-shaped back is decorated with a laurel wreath and a scrolling motif of inlaid ebony. Although the motifs vary, ebony inlay was a widely popular method of decorating furniture throughout Europe at this time. The laurel wreath and the icons' heads featured on the arm terminals both reflected the contemporary interest in classical archaeology.

RIGHT A small settee, or *causeuse*, which is part of a suite of furniture designed by the Jacob brothers in 1808. The suite, consisting of a bed, this settee with its accompanying footstool and a number of armchairs, was in a room used by the Empress Josephine in the *petits appartements* at Fontainebleau.

RIGHT Empire chairs tended to be very much heavier, more ample and less mobile than Louis XVI examples. Seats and backs, as in this richly gilt and upholstered armchair, are generally square in shape. These armchairs were often made *en suite*, with small footstool sofas and even matching firescreens. This one was made for the *petits appartements* at Fontainebleau to a design by P. G. Brion.

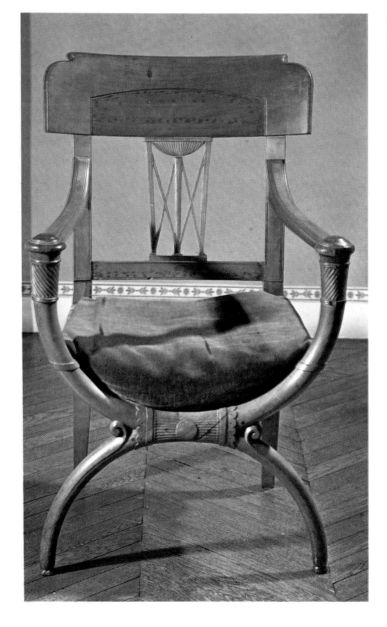

LEFT This simple mahogany chair is modelled on the ancient Roman camp stool, called a curule, and may have been made after a design by the court architects, Percier and Fontaine. The nailmarks on the back of the chair show where it has at some stage been upholstered, although the upholstery has since been removed and replaced with a more appropriate splat depicting a classical perfume burner.

LEFT   Despite its early Neoclassical type of decoration in the form of paterae and fluting, the severely rectilinear outline of this firescreen looks forward to the later Empire style.

BELOW   A mahogany *lit en bateau* which formed part of the furniture in the rooms occupied by Pope Pius VII at Fontainebleau.

NEAR RIGHT   The outline of this *bas d'armoire d'armoire* (under cupboard) in which the surface of mahogany is broken only by the ormolu wreaths of oak leaves, lacks the heroic monumentality associated with later Empire furniture.

FAR RIGHT   This commode, of the early Empire period, is in mahogany, which up to the time of the Continental Blockade in 1806 was much admired for its dark, rich tones and highly polished surface. Ormolu decoration was minimal and lion motifs were common. This example rests on finely carved lions' paws and the handles are formed by lion masks holding rings.

BELOW RIGHT   This severely tectonic commode veneered in a well figured mahogany, sometimes known as 'plum pudding' was made by C. Lemarchand in the first decade of the Empire period and is given added strength by being mounted on a solid plinth.

LEFT   This carved and gilded wall bracket (*appliqué*) was supplied to the Empress Joséphine at Malmaison.

BELOW LEFT   This *secrétaire* was made by the cabinet-maker Bennemann to a design by the Empire architects, Percier and Fontaine.

BELOW RIGHT   A delicate lady's writing-cabinet on stand, similar in design to those of Thomas Sheraton. Sheraton greatly popularized the use of striking colour and pattern combinations in his designs. Here, the satinwood veneer contrasts strongly with the small oval medallions of yew wood. This type of writing-cabinet is similar to the French *bonheur du jour* which was one of several types of light writing- and dressing-tables familiar in late eighteenth-century households.

ABOVE   An oval medallion on the front of the *secrétaire* shown above, depicting a reclining figure believed to symbolize learning. The fine marquetry decoration is of ebony and various fruit-woods against a ground of amaranth.

ABOVE LEFT   After the Continental Blockade of 1806, mahogany, which had formerly been imported largely from the British Colonies of America (now the West Indies), was virtually impossible to acquire. Furniture-makers were forced to use local and indigenous timbers, often with very pleasing and imaginative results. This elegant table, supported on graceful patinated X-shaped legs, is veneered in burr elm which provides a rich textural background to the simple ormolu mounts. The table, attributed to Thomire, is a combined writing- and dressing-table, but this form was also used as a games table.

ABOVE RIGHT   This satinwood fall-front *secrétaire* is closely based on the French type called a *secrétaire à abattant* and is a rare instance of this form being used in England. The delicate diaper motif along the frieze is another reference to the French source and is not typical of other work by Thomas Chippendale, who was responsible for supplying this piece to Harewood House in Yorkshire.

RIGHT   One of a set of ten dining chairs designed in about 1767 by Robert Adam for the banker Robert Child at Osterley Park, and possibly made by John Linnell. This is one of the earliest examples to have the graceful lyre-shaped pattern, here incorporated in the back, which was used in Europe, notably France, some fifteen years later.

BELOW   Oval and heart-shaped chair-backs, illustrated by George Hepplewhite in his *Cabinet Maker and Upholsterer's Guide* (1788) reached the height of their popularity during the 1780s. The oval back had already appeared in many of Adam's designs some ten years earlier, and by the 1790s was already outmoded in favour of the more rectilinear forms being introduced by Thomas Sheraton. The shield shape remained popular for a little longer and like the other two designs was subject to a wide variety of interpretations. The chair on the right is of painted satinwood and is one of a set of eighteen made by George Seddon's firm in 1790.

ABOVE LEFT   One of a set of fourteen parlour chairs made for Dyrham Park in about 1795, showing clear signs of French Directoire influence in the tablet-shaped back rail and the rounded form of the seat. The expeditions made by the French during the 1790s did much to stimulate interest in archaeology around the turn of the century. In this chair archaeological finds inspired the pattern of the back, which is similar to the tripod form of ancient perfume burners, and the painting *en grisaille* of putti along the back rail.

ABOVE RIGHT   A set of twelve armchairs, of which this is one, was made by Thomas Chippendale the younger for Sir Richard Colt Hoare in 1802. Despite Sheraton's obvious influence, as in the choice of contrasting woods (satinwood inlaid with lines of ebony), the chair also shows the heavier more masculine and simplified line of the Grecian style popular during the Regency. Sir Richard was a celebrated and respected antiquarian, and he took great interest in such details.

LEFT   A so-called 'Etruscan' chair, modelled on the type of decoration found on ancient pots which were long held to be Etruscan, but which have since been found to be of ancient Greek origin. The colouring of terracotta and black on a ground of greenish-grey was in imitation of the ancient vases which Adam used as the basic theme for the overall interior colour scheme. Part of a larger set of eight chairs, it is of painted pine and has a caned seat covered by a cushion.

ABOVE   This library table is one of the finest
examples of Chippendale's work and was made in his
workshops in about 1770 for Harewood House.
Chippendale must have employed the finest craftsmen
available to execute this superb marquetry and the
ormolu mounts, but little is known of his employees.
By the 1770s light-coloured woods such as satinwood
and rosewood had replaced mahogany, and these
provided an excellent background for the marquetry
which succeeded carving as the most popular form of
decoration.

LEFT   A detail of the above showing the variety of
superbly executed Neoclassical decoration in inlay and
mounts.

Glossary of Terms

ACANTHUS LEAF Stylized, deeply serrated leaf used in classical ornament and on all forms of European decorative arts.

ANTHEMION Floral motif based on the honeysuckle deriving from ancient Greek and Roman decoration but much used in Europe and America throughout the Neoclassical revival.

APRON Shaped and sometimes decorated section of wood immediately beneath table top, chair seat, chest-of-drawers or stand stretching between the legs and sometimes joining the legs at the rail joint.

ARABESQUE Motif of ancient Middle Eastern origin consisting of formalized leaf patterns interlaced with abstract scrolling lines.

ARM PAD Small padded section on arm of a chair.

ARMOIRE French term for wardrobe, cupboard or clothes-press.

ATHÉNIENNE Form of small table or pedestal based on ancient classical perfume burners with tripod stand. Said to derive its name from the painting entitled 'La Vertueuse Athénienne' by J. B. Vien showing incense being burnt at an altar on a three-legged support.

BACKSTOOL Term applied in the seventeenth and eighteenth centuries to a type of side or single chair characterized by a square, upholstered back, with a gap between the seat and back support.

BAS RELIEF Carved or moulded low relief ornamentation usually depicted within medallions, panels or friezes.

BEADING Ornamental moulding of semi-spherical form resembling beads.

BERGÈRE French term for a deep comfortable armchair with upholstered or caned sides and back. In England bergère was corrupted to 'burjairs', 'barjairs' and even 'barjier'.

BEVELLED GLASS A narrow, shallow cut slanting border around a panel of mirror plate.

BLOCK FRONT Form used in conjunction with case furniture, such as chests-of-drawers, bookcases or cabinets where the centre section either projects forwards or is recessed behind the side sections. Generally associated with eighteenth-century American furniture particularly that made in New England.

BOISERIE Carved wooden panelling used for interior wall decoration and generally painted or gilded.

BOMBÉ Bulging, outward swelling shape used particularly on case furniture such as commodes, in the Rococo style. The term is French and means 'blown out'.

BONHEUR DU JOUR Small popular form of writing cabinet fitted with a superstructure containing drawers and cubbyholes.

BOULLE WORK Takes its name from the famous ébéniste André-Charles Boulle, who worked under Louis XIV. He perfected a technique employing veneers of tortoiseshell and brass which was often combined with other materials such as silver, copper, pewter, mother-of-pearl and even stained horn, often set against a background of ebony. Two distinct forms emerged: in première-partie, the brass provides the principal pattern, set against a background of tortoiseshell. In contre-partie, the brass forms the background against which is set the tortoiseshell decoration. The term is now loosely used to indicate marquetry employing any of these materials. It is sometimes also described as 'buhl'.

BRACKET FOOT Short foot of rectangular form used for supporting the underframe of case furniture. It is sometimes carved and shaped.

BUN FOOT Ball-shaped foot of slightly flattened form.

BUREAU À CYLINDRE Type of desk particularly fashionable in France during the Louis XV and Louis XVI periods distinguished by a roll top in the form of a quarter cylinder.

BUREAU-CABINET A piece of furniture in two parts consisting of a bureau below and cabinet above. When the top section is intended to contain books, this is also called a bureau-bookcase. The cupboard doors can be panelled in wood, fitted with glass or mirrors.

BUREAU DE DAME Lady's writing desk popular during the third quarter of the eighteenth century in France. It is similar to the *bonheur du jour* but lacks the superstructure.

BUREAU PLAT A large flat-topped writing desk usually of rectangular form but sometimes with a serpentine outline and generally fitted with three lateral drawers on two sides.

BURR A curiously formed knotted growth on the trunk or root of a tree formed by abnormal development. The highly figured wood that resulted was particularly favoured for veneering. Deliberate cutting, or pollarding, of tree branches produces the same effect.

CABRIOLE LEG Type of leg introduced in the early eighteenth century of curving form like a reverse 'S', curving outward at the knee, in below, and out again at the foot, and used on all kinds of furniture. From the Italian *capriole*, a goat.

CANAPÉ French term for sofa or settee.

CANTED Surface cut on a slant; bevelled or chamfered.

CARCASS The body of a piece of furniture to which veneers are applied.

CARTOUCHE Circular or shaped tablet often bearing an armorial device or inscription surrounded by scrolls and leaves. Generally used as the focal point of carved decoration or used to highlight structural details such as the centre of a pediment or the knee of a cabriole leg.

CARYATID Decorative female figures in columnar form used to support a moulding or entablature. From the Greek 'maidens of Caryae' who danced at the festival of Artemis.

CHAISE VOLANTE A lightweight chair which could be moved easily; literally a 'flying chair'.

CHEST-ON-CHEST A chest-of-drawers with another chest-of-drawers supported above.

CHEVAL GLASS A type of looking-glass of rectangular form pivoted between two uprights. Introduced towards the end of the eighteenth century, these swing mirrors were called 'Psyches' in France after the mythological maiden beloved of Cupid.

CISELEURS-DOREURS French guild of craftsmen responsible for gilding the elaborate metal mounts used on furniture in the seventeenth and eighteenth centuries. Their great rival was the guild of the *fondeurs-ciseleurs* who cast and chased the mounts ready for gilding.

CLAW AND BALL FOOT Foot used in conjunction with the cabriole leg in the form of a paw or claw clutching a ball. It is sometimes held to derive from the dragon holding a pearl of Chinese mythology. It was a popular design widely used in England, Holland and North America during the first half of the eighteenth century.

COIFFEUSE French term applied to both a type of fitted dressing table or an armchair with a top rail curved down at the back to allow the hair to be dressed.

COMMODE A type of chest-of-drawers used only in the principal rooms of a house and on which high quality decoration was frequently lavished during the eighteenth century. Not to be confused with the night-stool of the nineteenth century to which the Victorians gave the same name.

COMMODE À VANTAUX A chest-of-drawers enclosed by cupboard doors. The drawers may be replaced by open shelves.

CONSOLE TABLE A table intended to be placed along a wall and whose top was generally supported by brackets or consoles.

CONTRE-PARTIE *See* Boulle work.

COROMANDEL LACQUER A type of Chinese lacquer imported into Europe during the seventeenth and eighteenth centuries in which the design was deeply incised. The name derives from the Coromandel coast of India along which most of the trade vessels bearing the lacquer panels must have sailed.

CORNICE The top section of an entablature or a moulded section above a frieze.

CRESTING Carved and pierced wood decoration used to ornament tops of some case and seat furniture.

CROCKET Projecting ornament in the form of leaves or buds, found on Gothic architecture and furniture and its later revivals.

CUSHION MIRROR Mirror framed by a wide half-round moulding of a type fashionable during the late seventeenth century.

DENTIL Type of moulding in the form of small rectangular blocks with narrow spaces between.

DIAPER   Trellis or lozenge pattern.

DUCHESSE   Type of extended *bergère* capable of supporting the legs of the occupant. A *duchesse brisée* is composed of two or three separate sections incorporating two *bergères* and a stool which can be fitted between both or used singly on the end of one.

DUMB-WAITER   Type of stand incorporating two or more tiers intended to hold food and dining equipment. Generally of circular form and supported on a central pedestal with a tripod base. Fashionable during the eighteenth century.

ÉBÉNISTE   French term for a cabinet maker who specialized in the complex craft of applying veneers to case furniture, *ébénisterie*. Not to be confused with the craft of the *menuisier*, who specialized in carving and joinery.

EBONIZED WOOD   Wood veneered with ebony. It can also mean inferior or cheaper woods which are stained in imitation of ebony.

EGG AND DART   Carved decorative mouldings consisting of raised alternate dart and oval motifs.

ENCOIGNURE   Small triangular commode designed to fit into a corner and frequently made to match a commode.

ENTABLATURE   The architrave, frieze and cornice found above a column or solid structure used in classical architecture.

ETAGÈRE   A piece of furniture consisting of a number of open shelves designed to display ornaments. Introduced in the late eighteenth century, they were either free standing or designed as wall fitments, often fitting into the corner of a room.

FALL-FRONT   Writing flap of a desk or bureau designed to fall flat to form a writing surface. Also known as a drop-front.

FAUTEUIL   French term for armchair distinguished from the *bergère* by having a space between the arms and seat. Generally upholstered, they were sometimes caned.

FAUTEUIL À LA REINE   This armchair, named as a compliment to Louis XV's Queen, Marie Lesczynska, has a flat rectangular back. It was fashionable during the second half of the eighteenth century.

FAUTEUIL EN CABRIOLET   An armchair slightly smaller than the *fauteuil à la reine* with a slightly curved back.

FIELDED PANEL   A slightly raised panel with bevelled edges.

FILLET   A narrow flat band often used between mouldings and sometimes gilded.

FINIAL   Decorative knob often in the form of an urn used to crown the ending of a structural feature.

FLUTING   Shallow concave parallel grooves often used to ornament classical columns and friezes. *Cf.* Reeding.

FRETWORK   Angular, abstract patterns often of geometric form cut or pierced to form a repetitive pattern around a gallery or on legs and stretchers of chairs and tables. Blind fretwork is a similar decoration carved or applied in low relief against a solid background.

FRIEZE   Central division of an entablature and below a cornice.

GENRE PITTORESQUE   Type of decoration based on fantastical elements drawn from nature including plant forms, water, rocks, vegetation, asymmetrical shellwork motifs (rocaille) and imaginary buildings and ruins. It was especially popular during the Rococo period.

GESSO   Composition used as a foundation for gilding and silvering on furniture, often consisting of gypsum and parchment size. Also used for modelling.

GILDING   The application of gold leaf to a surface.

GIRANDOLE   By the eighteenth century in England this term was generally applied to a type of wall light ornamented by a carved wood frame fitted with a mirror. In France it was more often used to describe a chandelier.

GRIFFIN   In Greek mythology, a monster with the body of a lion and the head of an eagle.

GUÉRIDON   French term for a candlestand introduced during the reign of Louis XIV. In the eighteenth century these were also used as small tables.

GUILLOCHE   Ornament of classical derivation consisting of interlaced circles sometimes enclosing foliate rosettes.

HIGHBOY   Contemporary American term for a high chest deriving from the English eighteenth-century tallboy.

HOOF FEET   Type of terminal used on early eighteenth-century cabriole legs, resembling an animal's hoof. In France these are known as *pied de biche*.

INLAY   Decoration of a surface, usually wooden, by insetting different coloured woods or other materials directly into the solid carcass.

INTARSIA   Italian term used to describe marquetry or inlay, whether geometric or pictorial.

JAPAN WORK   English term used to describe imitation lacquer work. Elsewhere imitation of oriental lacquer was described as *vernis Martin* (France) and *lacca* (Italy).

KLISMOS CHAIR   Type of chair of classical Greek origin. Characterized by a broad, deeply curved yoke or tablet-shaped back. It was revived during the early nineteenth century.

LACQUER   Method of decorating surfaces available only from the orient – China and Japan. It consisted of a type of varnish based on the gum of the lac-tree which would be applied in a number of layers to form a thick covering sheet to be decorated with motifs.

LAMBREQUIN   Ornament consisting of deeply scalloped border, deriving from heraldic decoration but used in wood, particularly during the late seventeenth century.

LIT À LA COLONNE   Tester of a bed supported by columns.

LIT À LA DUCHESSE   Tester of a bed suspended from the ceiling or by cantilevered supports.

LIT À LA FRANÇAISE   Traditional French four-poster bed where the tester is supported by the four posts and the head and foot boards.

LIT À LA POLONAISE   Four-poster bed with a small oval or circular canopy in the centre, all elaborately upholstered.

LIT EN BATEAU   A bed with boat-shaped ends.

MARCHAND-MERCIER   A dealer in the decorative arts, such as furniture, textiles and porcelain.

MARLBOROUGH LEG   English term for straight, square-cut leg sometimes chamfered on the inside corner, often associated with American furniture from the mid-eighteenth century onward. The leg sometimes terminates in a square plinth.

MARQUETRY   Surface decoration consisting of a variety of woods or other material cut into a variety of interlocking patterns, like a jigsaw puzzle, and veneered on to the carcass.

MENUISIER   Furniture-maker specializing in carving and joinery and producing chairs, looking-glass- and picture-frames, beds and tables. To be distinguished from the *ébéniste*.

MONOPODIUM (-IA)   Support of classical origin consisting of an animal's head and body with a single leg and foot. The lion was most commonly used.

MOULDING   Raised band or edging generally decorated with a repeat pattern often of classical derivation.

OGEE MOULDING   Motif of Gothic origin consisting of a double curve, concave above and convex below. Often used to form an 'ogee' shaped arch during the eighteenth-century Gothic revival.

ORMOLU   English term used to describe gilt bronze or brass metal mounts used on furniture. Although of French origin the term is not used in France, where *bronze doré* is preferred. 'Gilt bronze' is sometimes used in England.

OVOLO MOULDING   Decorative band of convex, quarter-circle form.

OYSTER VENEER   Whorl-patterned veneers cut from small branches and laid side-by-side and resembling oyster shells.

PAD FOOT   Widely used terminal found on cabriole legs, looking like a club foot set on a disc.

PALMETTE   Stylised spread palm leaf decoration of classical origin sometimes resembling an open fan.

PARQUETRY   Veneered geometric patterns.

PATERA (-AE)   Carved, painted inlaid or applied circular ornament of classical origin.

PEMBROKE TABLE   A lightweight table, usually attractively decorated, with two flaps which can be spread out horizontally and supported by four legs. Popular in the late eighteenth and early nineteenth centuries, it was named after the Countess of Pembroke who may have suggested the design.

PIETRE DURE   Marble ground, set with a mosaic of precious and semi-precious stones. The technique originated in Florence during the sixteenth century. It was used for decorating table tops, and giving a sumptuous appearance to cabinets.

PREMIÈRE-PARTIE   *See* Boulle work.

PRIE DIEU   Small individual kneeling desk for prayer, later adapted to a chair form and used for the same purpose.

QUATRE FOIL   Motif derived from medieval Gothic window tracery consisting of a four-lobed flower-head.

REEDING   Opposite of fluting. Formed by a series of convex mouldings resembling reeds.

ROUNDEL   Ornament consisting of any circular wreath or moulding in a variety of materials, such as porcelain, wood, metal, ivory or enamel, set into furniture.

SABRE LEG   Leg shaped like a sabre and much used during the early nineteenth century. Sometimes called a scimitar leg.

SCAGLIOLA   Composition of plaster, marble chips and glue which when set was very hard and capable of taking a very high polish. Used to imitate marble and other ornamental stone such as *pietre dure*.

SCONCE, WALL SCONCE   Wall light.

SEAWEED MARQUETRY Type of marquetry popular in the Netherlands and England during the late seventeenth and early eighteenth centuries, consisting of arabesque patterns with scrolls and tendrils.

SECRÉTAIRE Writing desk with a vertical hinged drop front that falls down to provide a writing surface.

SECRÉTAIRE À ABATTANT A *secrétaire* in which the drop front opens to reveal drawers and pigeonholes. Usually fitted below with a cupboard, concealing shelves or drawers.

SERPENTINE LINE A line consisting of two concave curves centring on a convex one. According to Hogarth this was the line of beauty.

SIÈGE Chair without arms; either caned or upholstered. A *siège courant* could be moved around the room; a *siège meublant* was intended to be stationary.

SPLAT Vertical central member in the back of a chair, running between the top rail and the seat rail and often shaped or pierced.

STRAPWORK Carved surface ornament composed of interlacing curling bands and straps popular during the late sixteenth and seventeenth centuries.

STRETCHER Horizontal bar uniting and strengthening the legs on chairs and tables.

STRINGING Narrow lines of wood and sometimes ivory on metal inlaid into a piece of furniture for decoration.

SWAG Looped decoration composed of fabric or flowers, fruit and foliage, often caught at either end into a pendant festoon.

TABLE AMBULANTE Small, light moveable table.

TABOURET Upholstered stool standing on four legs.

TAMBOUR FRONT Roll front used for desks consisting of thin strips of wood glued to a canvas backing.

TESTER Canopy used mainly to cover beds but also above throne chairs.

TOP RAIL Top horizontal member of a chair.

TORCHÈRE Another term for a portable candlestand or *guéridon*.

TREFOIL Three-lobed ornament.

TRUMEAU French term for pier glass, made to fit between windows on the pier wall.

TURNING Method of decorating columns of wood mainly used as legs on tables and chairs. Executed on a pole lathe, a machine which was foot-operated until mechanization came in during the later nineteenth century. A wide variety of patterns developed including the bobbin twist, spiral twist (also known as 'barley sugar' twist), ball and reel turning; the baluster turned column was probably the most widely used variant. Turning originated in ancient Greece but enjoyed its greatest popularity in the seventeenth century.

VEILLEUSE Type of sofa with a continuous back forming a high end and descending to a low one.

VENEERING Method of glueing thin sheets of wood, usually of an exotic or well-figured kind, to a solid carcass, for decoration.

VERNIS MARTIN French term for varnishing or lacquering furniture. The method was patented by the four Martin brothers in 1730 and was very popular throughout the eighteenth century. It is also used to describe imitations of Chinese lacquer.

VOLUTE Deep spiral scroll motif especially associated with the Ionic capital which consists of two volutes placed back to back in profile.

VITRUVIAN SCROLL Ornament also known as wavy-line pattern. Consisting of a line of convoluted scrolls.

VOYEUSE Chair with a padded top rail sometimes fitted with arms.

WINE CELLERET Term used to describe a wine cooler or a deep drawer in a sideboard fitted to hold a number of bottles.

WINE TABLE Modern term used to describe low, small, tripod tables most probably originally intended for use as kettle stands.

Development of Styles

The names that we use for styles of furniture are useful for the purpose of immediate identification, but can often be misleading. The following pages show the sequence of styles of Western furniture during the seventeenth, eighteenth and early nineteenth centuries, which will enable the reader to recognize the outlines of each of the most important types of furniture.

Baroque

Baroque furniture derives from the highly dramatic architecture and sculpture of the period; the total effect is both monumental and restless, although most Baroque furniture is essentially symmetrical in design.

Case furniture

Initially the most important piece of European case furniture was the Italian *cassone*, embellished with classical curves, rounded arches and carytids. In England and North America the term coffer was used. Towards the end of this period the cabinet (with drawers, derived from Chinese originals) was developed, bringing a new sophistication to the decoration of case furniture in the hands of the *ébéniste* and the *ciseleur*.

It will be apparent that there is no abrupt distinction between pieces of, say, the Baroque and Rococo periods, for designers, however sophisticated, very rarely dropped one style totally to replace it with another, and the unsophisticated craftsman working many miles from the capital often followed styles years or even decades after they had ceased to be fashionable in the big city.

3 Sixteenth-century Italian cupboard influenced by contemporary architecture.

1 Late fifteenth-century Italian chest in the form of a sarcophagus.

2 Sixteenth-century Italian chest heavily decorated with carving.

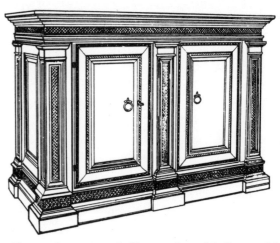

4 Seventeenth-century Italian cabinet-on-stand in the form of a miniature palace.

5 Late seventeenth-century French elaborate cabinet-on-stand.

7 Early eighteenth-century Dutch bureau-bookcase.

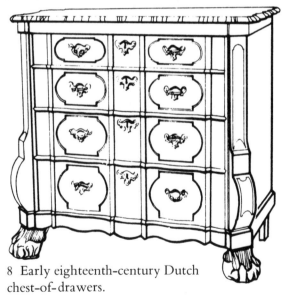

6 Late seventeenth-century Germanic cupboard.

8 Early eighteenth-century Dutch chest-of-drawers.

Seat furniture

Social change in the early seventeenth century brought a new rich class into being, which demanded not only comfort but ostentation. Nevertheless chairs in a more restrained style continued to be found in the same houses. Many chairs were richly upholstered with tapestry and leather, silk and velvet, and their designs gradually became more fanciful. Gilding was fashionable, particularly in Europe.

1 Fifteenth-century Italian stool of traditional design.

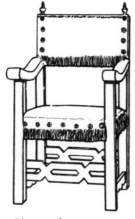

2 Sixteenth-century Italian armchair, with innovatory decorative carving on the stretchers.

3 Mid-seventeenth-century French armchair.

4 Eighteenth-century Italian chair frame.

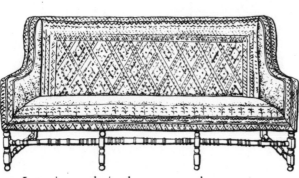

5 Late sixteenth-/early seventeenth-century Germanic settee.

6 Late seventeenth-century Dutch chair.

7 Early eighteenth-century English Georgian chair.

Tables and Desks

Tables were an important part of formal arrangements in reception rooms. The legs gave sculptors a magnificent opportunity for carving in great depth and hook-like scrolls gradually replaced the vertical lines.

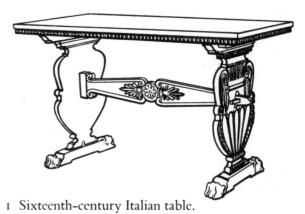

1 Sixteenth-century Italian table.

2 Seventeenth-century Italian desk.

3 Early eighteenth-century English Queen Anne table.

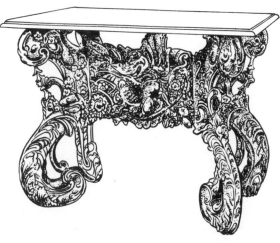

6 Late seventeenth-century Dutch table.

4 Seventeenth-century Italian table showing the strong influence of Bernini.

7 Late seventeenth-century Germanic table (from Danzig).

Beds and other furniture

Four-poster beds persisted for hundreds of years because in many countries the idea of a bedroom as such was unknown until the eighteenth century. Other decorative items of the period included *guéridons* (candlestands) and mirrors, which reflected the lavish carving of every surface then prevailing.

5 Late seventeenth-century French suite of table, mirror and candlestands.

1 Late seventeenth-century French candlestands.

2 Mid-seventeenth-century French bed.

4 Late seventeenth-century Italian mirror frame.

Rococo

A reaction to the formality of Baroque decoration the Rococo is essentially light–almost frivolous–with delicate curving lines and a romantic flavour. It had a marked tendency towards asymmetry in its carvings.

Case furniture

The *bombé* shape dominates the smaller pieces, while almost all case furniture was flamboyantly decorated with marquetry, parquetry and *ormolu*.

3 Late seventeenth-century Dutch bed.

1 Mid-eighteenth-century Dutch cabinet-on-cabinet.

2 Mid-eighteenth-century French commode.

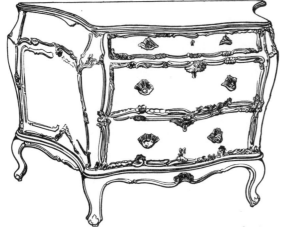

3 Eighteenth-century Italian *bombé* chest-of-drawers.

5 Eighteenth-century Italian bureau-cabinet.

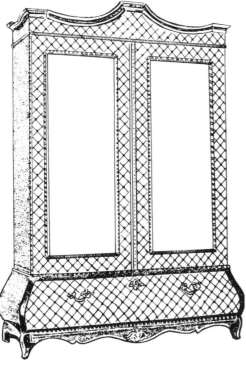

4 Mid-eighteenth-century Dutch clothes-press.

6 Mid-eighteenth-century Germanic bureau-cabinet.

Seat furniture

A whole range of elegant but comfortable seat furniture was developed during this period, uniformed by the essentially feminine character of the style. Notable features include the S-shaped leg, ribband-back carving on chair backs, chinoiserie and upward-scrolling feet. The wood was sometimes gilded, sometimes painted, and sometimes left its natural colour and waxed.

1 Mid-eighteenth-century German settee.

7 Mid-eighteenth-century Germanic china-cabinet.

2 Mid-eighteenth-century Louis XV armchair.

3 Mid-eighteenth-century English ribband-back chair.

8 Mid-eighteenth-century English chinoiserie china-cabinet.

4 Eighteenth-century Italian settee in gondola form, of Piedmont and Venice.

5 Mid-eighteenth-century French settee.

2 Mid-eighteenth-century Italian console table.

6 Mid-eighteenth-century French caned chair.

3 Mid-eighteenth-century French console table.

Tables and desks

Tables and desks of this period feature flowing lines, delicate C-scrolls, floral motifs and acanthus leaves, which – in association with the cabriole leg and the English and American claw-and-ball foot – make up the repertoire of the Rococo.

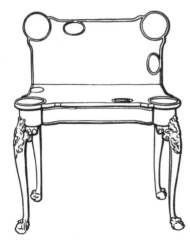

1 Mid-eighteenth-century English games table.

4 Mid-eighteenth-century French lady's writing table.

5 Mid-eighteenth-century English pedestal table.

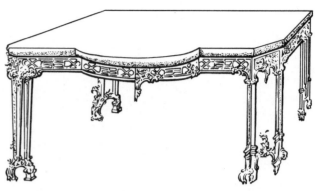

8 Mid-eighteenth-century design for a table by Thomas Chippendale.

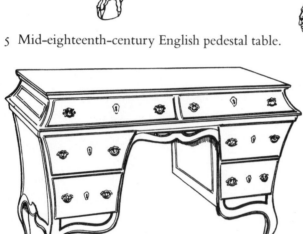

6 Mid-eighteenth-century Italian kneehole desk.

9 Mid-eighteenth-century Germanic table.

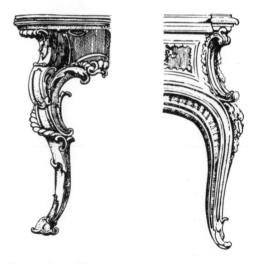

10 Examples of legs used on mid-eighteenth-century French tables.

7 Mid-eighteenth-century American desk.

Beds and other furniture

During this period the finest mahogany or fruitwoods were used for the most extravagant examples of asymmetrical carving. The Rococo vocabulary was applied to every conceivable surface.

Neoclassical

The Neoclassical style was inspired partly as a reaction to the excesses of the Rococo and partly by enthusiasm for the architecture and decoration of ancient Greece and Rome, which was particularly stimulated by excavations at Pompeii and Herculaneum.

Case furniture

The geometry and severe lines of the Neoclassical style are readily apparent in the case furniture of the period. The pieces are decorated with the Neoclassical language – urns, ram's heads, trophies of palms and scenes from mythology.

1 Mid-eighteenth-century French firescreens.

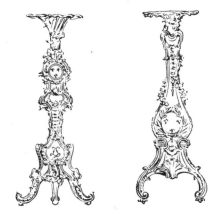

2 Mid-eighteenth-century French candlestands.

3 Mid-eighteenth-century Dutch bed.

1 Late eighteenth-century Germanic commode.

2 Late eighteenth-century Dutch clothes-press.

Seat furniture

Seat furniture was an ideal vehicle on which to reproduce Greek, Roman and Egyptian revival styles. Square, architecturally inspired armchairs with sabre or turned legs, scrolled arms and low backs were prevalent.

1 Late eighteenth-century English chair.

2 Late eighteenth-century Dutch armchair.

3 Late eighteenth-century Dutch fall-front writing desk.

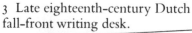

4 Late eighteenth-century (*c*.1775) Germanic commode.

3 Late eighteenth-century English shield-back armchair.

4 Late eighteenth-century Italian chair.

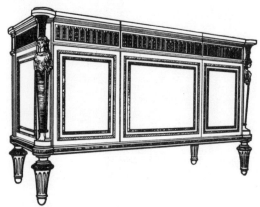

5 Late eighteenth-century French commode.

5 Early nineteenth-century Germanic settee.

6 Early nineteenth-century French cross-frame armchair.

2 Late eighteenth-century Italian writing desk.

7 Early nineteenth-century French sabre-leg chair.

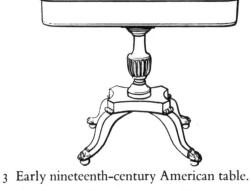

3 Early nineteenth-century American table.

Tables and desks

A large variety of tables was made during this period. The shapes of the legs varied from simple tapered to a turned centre column with four splayed feet, and the decoration was more severe. Curves were based on the circle, the oval and a simple serpentine.

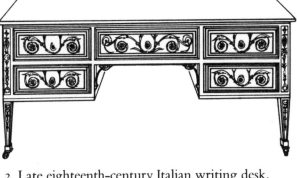

4 Late eighteenth-century Italian console table.

1 Late eighteenth-century Austrian lady's writing-table.

5 Late eighteenth-century French table.

6 Late eighteenth-century American table.

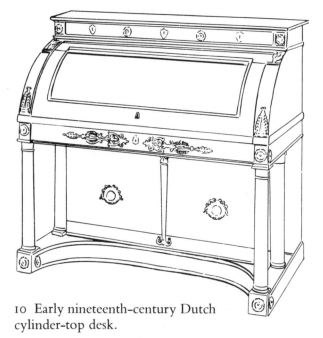

9 Late eighteenth-century Italian pedestal table.

7 Late eighteenth-century English Pembroke table.

10 Early nineteenth-century Dutch cylinder-top desk.

8 Early nineteenth-century English sofa table.

11 Late eighteenth-century English dumb-waiter.

12 Examples of legs used on late eighteenth-century French tables.

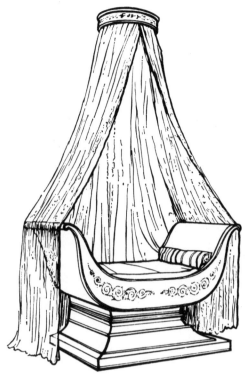

I Early nineteenth-century French bed.

13 Examples of female-figure table supports used on early nineteenth-century French furniture.

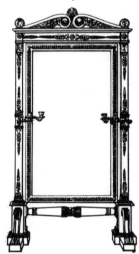

2 Early nineteenth-century French cheval glass.

Beds and other furniture

Details from the designs of the ancient world were represented wherever possible on Neoclassical pieces. These included caryatids and shields, and the shapes as well as the ornaments were essentially faithful to the originals.

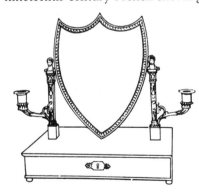

3 Early nineteenth-century French toilet mirror.

Bibliography

Aprà, Netta *The Empire Style 1804-1815* (London, 1972).

Aprà, Netta *The Louis Styles* (London, 1972).

Ayres, James *American Antiques* (London, 1973).

Baker, H. S. *Furniture in the Ancient World* (London, 1966).

Bjerkoe, E. H. *The Cabinetmakers of America* (New York, 1957).

Blunt, Anthony *Art & Architecture in France 1500-1700* (Harmondsworth, 1973).

Charlish, Anne (ed.) *The History of Furniture* (London, 1976).

Chinnery, V. *Oak Furniture: The British Tradition* (Woodbridge, 1980).

Chippendale, Thomas *The Gentleman and Cabinet-maker's Director* (London, 1754).

Copplestone, T. *World Architecture* (London, 1963).

Comstock, H. *American Furniture: Seventeenth, Eighteenth and Nineteenth Century Styles* (New York, 1962).

Davis, Terence *Rococo: a Style of Fantasy* (London, 1973).

Downs, J. *American Furniture of the Queen Anne and Chippendale Periods in the Henry Francis Du Pont Winterthur Museum* (New York, 1952).

Eberlein, H. D. *Interiors, Fireplaces and Furniture of the Italian Renaissance* (New York, 1916).

Edwards, R. *The Shorter Dictionary of English Furniture* (Feltham, 1964).

Eriksen, S. *Early Neo-Classicism in France* (London, 1974).

Fastnedge, Ralph *English Furniture Styles 1500-1830* (Harmondsworth, 1955).

Girouard, Marc *Life in the English Country House* (New Haven and London, 1978).

Gloag, J. (ed.) *A Short Dictionary of Furniture* (London, 1964).

Grandjean, S. *Empire Furniture* (London, 1966).

Gilbert, C. *The Life and Work of Thomas Chippendale* (London, 1978).

Harris, E. *The Furniture of Robert Adam* (London, 1963).

Hayward, H. (ed.) *World Furniture* (Feltham, 1969).

Honour, H. *Cabinet Makers and Furniture Designers* (London, 1969).

Jourdain, M. *English Interior Decoration 1500-1830* (London, 1950).

Joy, Edward T. *English Furniture 1800-1851* (London, 1977).

Kenworthy-Browne, John *Chippendale and his Contemporaries* (London, 1973).

Montgomery, C. *American Furniture of the Federal Period* (Delaware, 1967).

Miller, E. G., Jr. *American Antique Furniture* (2 vols, New York, 1966).

Odom, W. M. *A History of Italian Furniture from the 14th to the Early 19th Centuries* (2 vols, New York 1918-19).

Praz, Mario *An Illustrated History of Interior Decoration from Pompeii to Art Nouveau* (London, 1964).

de Ricci, S. *Louis XVI Furniture* (London, 1913).

Rosenberg, J., Seymour, S., Kuile, E. H. *Dutch Art and Architecture 1600-1800* (Harmondsworth, 1977).

Scarisbrick, Diana *Baroque: The Age of Exuberance* (London, 1973).

Singleton, E. *Dutch and Flemish Furniture* (London and New York, 1907).

Symonds, R. W. *Furniture making in Seventeenth- and Eighteenth-century England* (London, 1955).

Summerson, Sir John *Architecture in Britain 1530-1830* (Harmondsworth, 1955).

Thornton, P. *Seventeenth-Century Interior Decoration in England, France and Holland* (New Haven and London, 1978).

Verlet, Pierre *French Furniture and Interior Decoration of the 18th century* (London, 1967); *French Royal Furniture 1800-1825* (London, 1963); *French Royal Furniture* (London, 1963).

Ward-Jackson, P. *English Furniture Designs of the Eighteenth Century* (London, 1958).

Watkin, D. *Thomas Hope and the Neoclassical Ideal* (London, 1968).

Watson, F. J. B. *Louis XVI Furniture* (London, 1960).

Wittkower, Rudolf *Art and Architecture in Italy 1600-1750* (Harmondsworth, 1973).

Catalogues

de Bellaigue, G. *Furniture, Clocks and Gilt Bronzes in the James A. de Rothschild Collection at Waddesdon Manor* (Fribourg, 1974).

Watson, F. J. B. *Wallace Collection: Catalogue of Furniture* (Beccles, 1956).

Wrightsman Collection Catalogue (3 vols, New York, 1966).

Index

Acknowledgments

The furniture on pages 92b and 110 is reproduced by Gracious
Permission of H.M. Queen Elizabeth II. Other photographs
were supplied by: American Museum in Britain Bath, Baltimore
Museum of Art, Barroux Collection, Duke of Buccleuch &
Queensbury, Chateau de Champs, Christie Manson & Wood,
G. Dagli Orti, The Henry Francis du Pont Winterthur Museum,
Michael Holford Library, Archivio IGDA, A. F. Kersting,
Kunstmuseum Düsseldorf, Leeds City Art Gallery, Mallet &
Son, Metropolitan Museum of Art New York, Mount Vernon
Ladies Association of the Union, Musée d'Ansembourg, Musée
d'Art et de Ceramique Narbonne, Musée des Arts Décoratifs
Paris, Musée Condé Chantilly, Musée de Mariemont, Musée
National du Chateâu de Versailles, Musée de Poitiers, Musée de
Rheims, Museum of Fine Arts Boston, Museum für Kunst-
handwerk Frankfurt, National Trust, Duke of Northumber-
land, Österreichische Museum Vienna, F. Partridge, Residenz
Museum Munich, Rijksmuseum Amsterdam, Edwin Smith,
Soprintendenze ai Monumenti del Piemonte Turin, Sotheby
Parke Bernet, Victoria & Albert Museum, Wallace Collection,
White House Washington.